WRITING
SCIENCE FICTION
THAT
SELLS

WRITING
SCIENCE FICTION
THAT
SELLS

HARVEY L. BILKER & AUDREY L. BILKER

Library of Congress Cataloging in Publication Data

Bilker, Harvey L.
    Writing science fiction that sells.

    Includes index.
    1. Science fiction—Authorship.
I. Bilker, Audrey.   II. Title.
PN3377.5.S3B5   808'.02   81-69619
ISBN 0-8092-5823-4   AACR2

Published by Contemporary Books, Inc.
180 North Michigan Avenue, Chicago, Illinois 60601
Manufactured in the United States of America
Library of Congress Catalog Card Number: 81-69619
International Standard Book Number: 0-8092-5823-4

Published simultaneously in Canada by
Beaverbooks, Ltd.
150 Lesmill Road
Don Mills, Ontario M3B 2T5
Canada

Contents

Introduction   *vii*

PART I: WRITING SCIENCE FICTION

1. What Is Science Fiction?   *1*

2. Science Fiction Reading Sources   *13*

3. Ideas   *17*

4. Writing Tips   *29*

PART II: THE SCIENCE FICTION COMMUNITY

5. The Fans   *41*

6. The Pros   *47*

7. The Conventions   *51*

8. The S.F. Writers' Organizations   *57*

9. The Awards   *61*

10. Publications   *67*

PART III: THE PROFESSIONAL MANUSCRIPT— PREPARATION AND SUBMISSIONS

11. What Do Editors Look For?   *73*

12. Appearance, Format, and Length   *77*

13. Handling the Manuscript Pages   *85*

14. Querying the Editor   *89*

15. Submitting the Manuscript   *95*

16. The Publishers' Responses   *101*

PART IV: ACCEPTANCE AND BEYOND

17. Payment and Protection   *111*

18. Literary Representation   *119*

19. Legal and Financial Matters   *125*

20. Science Fiction Markets   *131*

    Index   *151*

Introduction

Within the last decade something wonderful happened to science fiction. It turned respectable. The genre became recognized as a literary form, a literature of ideas.

Seized upon by the academic field, courses for the study, as well as the writing, of science fiction have proliferated in universities, high schools, and grammar schools, and as night courses. Dissertations have been written about science fiction—the literature itself, its writers, philosophies, themes, history, and other aspects—and scholarly papers and journals have infiltrated the field of this popular genre.

Many book publishers who had never before considered publishing science fiction have entered the field, and more are following.

Slick magazines now publish a significant amount of science fiction. Articles about the genre and its writers appear in these popular periodicals, too.

Large magazine-publishing companies have established new

slick magazines to take advantage of the huge, growing readership. And some fan magazines have become professional and are available to the general public—no longer just within the science fiction community.

Science fiction books are now receiving more attention from major magazine and newspaper reviewers.

Mainstream writers are using the themes and techniques of science fiction. And so are other genre writers.

The entertainment field also has discovered quality science fiction. The film industry is now producing a steady stream of large-budget, high-quality (non-grade B) science fiction movies as a result of the popularity and great financial return of *Star Wars* and *Alien,* among others. These are films that transcend the science fiction movies of the past, reflecting in each fictional universe current trends and realism, as well as social patterns and current scientific knowledge.

Awards that have until recently been given only to mainstream fiction are now being conferred on science fiction authors and their works.

And, as a tribute to the popularity of the genre, the annual Academy of Science Fiction, Fantasy and Horror Films award ceremonies, like the Oscars, are telecast.

The phenomenal growth of science fiction has made it quite literally the fiction of the future, as well as often being fiction about the future.

Science fiction is a genre whose time has come. And you, as a writer, can be a part of it.

This book is your guide to the world of science fiction. In it you will learn the "secrets" of writing science fiction and, more importantly, the "secrets" of selling it!

In a behind-the-scenes glimpse of this unique literary universe, you will also be given explicit information in easy-to-understand terms about the entire range of this literature.

Part I includes a definition guide of the categories of science fiction, and step-by-step examples of exactly how to use these categories in the genre. In addition, you will learn where to find source materials, how to glean your ideas, the ways to employ them in your manuscripts, how to use your imagination creatively, yet within the bounds of the genre's rules, and other tips that can lead to your success as a science fiction writer.

Part II offers information about the science fiction community and its potential benefits to your writing career—the fascinating social world of science fiction where new and established writers meet informally with editors, publishers, and fans around the country and the world. You will learn how acquaintances are made, friendships are born, and careers in writing are started and advanced among the new aspiring writers in the midst of the established professional arena.

Part III of this book, "The Professional Manuscript—Preparation and Submissions," offers detailed information on how a professional manuscript is prepared, how to query an editor, follow up on a delayed response, and determine what the editors are looking for.

Because the business side of writing is so important for beginning writers, we've included a wealth of facts covering agents, contracts, copyright information, cover letters, and photocopied and multiple submissions. To guide you in selling your manuscripts, Part IV also gives complete and informative lists of markets of the science fiction genre, compiled especially for this book. Each specific market—for magazines, book publishers, and even anthology editors—gives detailed editorial requirements and facts on submissions that are available nowhere else. Additionally, source books and other publications that you can consult for even more markets are noted. Besides all of this, you'll learn where to look in the future for information about the upcoming needs of editors who will be looking to buy work from new authors.

In no other realm of today's fiction are editors buying more manuscripts—or are they more open to first sales—than in the genres. For that reason, we have put together this book for you, the aspiring writer, to guide you in writing and selling science fiction.

WRITING
SCIENCE FICTION
THAT
SELLS

PART I: WRITING
SCIENCE FICTION

1

What Is Science Fiction?

The term *science fiction* is abbreviated as *s.f.* in upper case or lower case letters, with or without periods. It is pronounced *ess eff*. In this book, science fiction will often be referred to as *s.f.*

To those within the s.f. community, the term *sci-fi* is repulsive because its use usually reveals a lack of knowledge of both the written genre and the s.f. community. However, this is the term with which the general public is most familiar because it is used in connection with movies and TV.

Although this book deals with the literary aspect of s.f.—short and long stories, novels, and poetry—the entire genre also encompasses the arts (including photography) and the entertainment fields of TV, films, theater, and radio.

Science fiction includes fantasy, though certain fantasy writing belongs to a separate category and may eventually become a separate genre as it continues to evolve. Horror is a double-genre category—that is, it is sometimes part of the mystery genre and sometimes part of s.f./fantasy.

Ask anyone who is knowledgeable about the genre—publisher, editor, reviewer, critic, writer, or fan—for an exact definition of science fiction, or any of its categories, and you will get a different answer from each person. A book or story may be described as hard or soft s.f., sword & sorcery, fantasy, or alternate history. An anthologist may request submissions of horror s.f. A writer may describe his or her work as speculative fiction. A reviewer may refer to a work as space opera or mainstream s.f. Since there is no agreement on exact definitions for these categores within the genre, the descriptions that follow are offered merely as a guide.

Science Fiction Definition Guide

Science Fiction

In general, science fiction deals with some aspect of technology or science, whether or not that particular technology or science exists at present or is an extrapolation or theory logically presented. It also includes the methodical and systematic investigation and/or study of any subject, whether or not investigation of that subject actually exists. A "false" science such as astrology is part of fantasy, not of s.f. But a scientific investigation of astrology would be s.f. Time travel and faster-than-light travel do not exist at present, and may never exist, but their concepts are based on actual sciences and scientific theories. Remember, space travel was considered impossible not too long ago.

Science fiction does not predict the future. It imaginatively extrapolates from what is known or theorized.

Whenever there is a new advance in science or technology, the media claim that "it's just like science fiction" or that we've finally "caught up" with science fiction. This is not true. As much as science fiction is set in the future, it does not predict it. The ideas in science fiction are far ahead of reality.

Science fiction is literature that, once its words and ideas grip the reader, opens up windows on our universe, allowing us to view it through the visions of the genre's creative minds, to see beyond the mundane realities of our everyday existence into the vast, yet undiscovered possibilities that man has the capacity and wherewithal to explore and harness.

There are two categories in the science part of s.f.—*hard* and *soft* s.f. The descriptions which follow of these terms are not meant to define hard science or soft science but to show how these sciences are used in science fiction. Basically, in hard science you can duplicate results—you get the same answer every time. In soft science the results are interpreted. But science fiction interprets all sciences, making the definitions of hard science and soft science misleading. Also, there are sciences that may, as used by science fiction, be both hard and soft, such as the medical sciences. It is how these sciences are used within a piece of fiction that determines the category.

Hard S.F.

In general, hard science fiction is about those sciences that deal with nonliving matter; sciences having laws, such as mathematics, physics, and chemistry; technology, such as spacecraft, time machines, and robots; engineering, such as in terraforming; outer space and the sciences pertaining to objects in it, which would include such subjects as solar dynamics, geology, mineralogy, meteorology, and especially astronomy and astrophysics; and the manufacturing of living organisms or life forms (cloning or genetic engineering) and human/animal, human/alien or human/mechanical combinations.

Soft S.F.

Soft science fiction is generally about those sciences that deal with living matter; life forms of any kind, whether human, animal, insect, microbe, or even alien; the results or effects of any science or technology on any life form; the interaction of life forms with each other or with their environment or with any science or technology; and any subject that is part of the human experience as applied to any life form. This broadly encompasses such areas as the humanities, and includes such subjects as the medical sciences, psychology, ecology, evolution, philosophy, archeology, anthropology, the arts and entertainment fields, economics, politics, the social sciences, and history—past, present, and future (but *not* alternate history).

Fantasy

In general, fantasy is more easily explained by what it is not. It is not based on any form of science or reality. Extrasensory perception (ESP) and other psychic powers, such as psi, are part of fantasy, though their study is part of s.f. Included in this category are astrology, all religious beliefs, mythology, legends, and magic or forces that appear to be magical. Magic is sometimes referred to as *hard fantasy*. Fantasy does not have to be logical, as s.f. must.

Alternate History

This is a subcategory of fantasy. A bit of the past is changed and all events of history from that point forward are altered drastically. Suppose England had won the Revolutionary War in 1776? What if Hitler had never been born? Suppose the South had won the Civil War? What if Karl Marx and his philosophies had never existed? The farther back in time you go, the more drastic the changes to the history that we know. If the Roman Empire had continued to exist, what would the world be like now?

Sword & Sorcery

This is a subcategory of hard fantasy and is sometimes called *heroic fantasy*. It deals generally and basically with the fight between good and evil, using magic or what appears to be magic. A hero, who fights with a sword, has a mission to perform. This task is usually referred to as a *quest* and along the way he has a great many adventures. In the end he duels with the evil sorcerer—and wins. In true *heroic fantasy,* there is no magic.

Horror

In the s.f. genre, horror is not necessarily in the realm of the supernatural and macabre. It usually includes any of the themes in the fantasy category (not the fantasy subcategories, such as alternate history), written in a manner to frighten the reader. *Gothic horror* refers to the style of writing of classic horror writers, such as Poe and Derleth.

Space Opera

Basically adventure science fiction, space opera employs any elements of hard or soft s.f. or s.f.–fantasy or even sword and sorcery without being overtly evident as having been taken from the sword & sorcery subcategory of fantasy. There is always a hero or heroine. "Flash Gordon" and "Buck Rogers" are excellent examples of space opera.

Speculative Fiction

This is not a true category, but a term used by writers to keep their work from being labeled science fiction. (The designation *s.f.* conveniently covers both science fiction and speculative fiction.) Whether speculative fiction uses as a background any hard or soft science fiction or fantasy–science fiction, its main focus is the human or psychological element—though the story may not necessarily involve human beings. And the science, if utilized at all, may be faulty. However, removal of the science fiction elements can result in a collapse of the story. The style of writing may be almost poetic. But any form of fiction—not just science fiction—can be called speculative fiction.

There is a growing trend to label certain visual/dramatic presentations as *speculation* and to use this label for science fiction as well. This type of writing is not speculative fiction, but a vastly different category that is not a part of science fiction. *Speculation* can also apply to books classified as nonfiction. Speculation might better be described as *conjecture.* In speculation, certain objects or occurrences are depicted as mysterious, and opinions are given without any solid evidence to substantiate any theories. And the supposed solution to the "mystery" is usually "visitors from outer space."

Mainstream S.F.

This category is written for the general public, not for readers of science fiction. Mainstream s.f., like speculative fiction, uses a science fiction background and concentrates on human drama. But, if the s.f. component is removed from the mainstream s.f. story, and any non–s.f. component is substituted, the story will not collapse.

Miscellaneous Labels

Space Western or *Gothic science fiction,* and other terms are sometimes applied to works that are basically s.f. In this type of fiction, the entire story line and background setting could easily be of a non-science-fiction genre, such as a Western. This does not make the story any less science fiction merely because the literary devices used in Westerns are in the s.f. story. These types of stories are unintentional mixed genres.

Mixed-Genre

In this type science fiction or fantasy is combined with a different genre. The mystery genre is the one most often combined and can be used quite successfully. Unfortunately, a true mixture of genres, with each genre true to its own literary rules, is very rare. The s.f./mystery story, published in an s.f. magazine, might not follow the rules of the mystery genre. Likewise, a mystery/s.f. story in a mystery genre magazine may contain flawed science fiction, perhaps with a theme that hasn't been used since the pulp days of s.f., or greatly faulted science.

Double-Genre

This category is claimed by both genres of which it is comprised. The only double-genre in science fiction is horror, which is also a category in the mystery genre. The double nature of horror—the fact that it remains true to the criteria of both genres—makes its stories publishable in the magazines of either genre, unless the story is overtly s.f.

This definition guide should help you understand what you read and can assist you in story writing.

A Sample Story Line Using All the Categories

Exactly what makes a story hard or soft science fiction or fantasy and relegates it to a specific category of s.f.? To explain these varying factors, let's use a single story line:

> Three spacemen are sent on a mission to orbit a planetary body and observe it for future exploration. Suddenly, while nearly halfway to their destination, there is a malfunction aboard the spacecraft. The lives of the crew are in jeopardy. The mission is aborted and, after a perilous return voyage, the crew returns home safely.

If this story seems familiar, it is because this is the true story of the Apollo astronauts whose disastrous mission was reported by the news media. But it also can be science fiction or fantasy with a few changes in the actual event.

Below are examples of how this story can be altered to fit different science fiction categories:

Mainstream S.F.

The story might be fictionalized through a slight change in

time—a few years before or after the actual event's date. Or it could become an international cooperative venture, with the crew members hailing from three countries of different political ideologies. Perhaps one or more of the crew could be female. The story would center around the interaction among the crew members, the reaction on Earth of the various other personnel involved in the mission, relatives of the astronauts, and the countries, their leaders, and their citizens. Technical or scientific aspects of the story would be downplayed. This would put the story into the "disaster" category of mainstream s.f., since the vehicle could easily be an airplane or a train, and the story would remain the same. Merely using an s.f. background does not make this story true science fiction. Such a story would probably be rejected by the genre magazines, unless it was written by a well-known mainstream writer or a big-name s.f. author. It might be a sale to some general fiction magazine, or it could be done as a novel.

Hard S.F.

The true story itself is hard s.f., because it contains space travel, technology, and sciences with definite laws, such as mathematics and physics. But it can be fictionalized, keeping it within the hard s.f. category, with a variety of changes. The planetary body wouldn't be the moon, but a planet in our solar system or in a different solar system in this or another galaxy. All the crew members wouldn't necessarily be human; they could be human and alien, all aliens (but not exploring the Earth), robots, or a mixture of all three entities. The story could take place in the future, no matter how distant, or in the past— especially if it is in the aliens' past. The physical appearance of the spacecraft and its method of propulsion would be different. Its speed could be faster than light. It might even travel from one universe to another. The crew might have been traveling for centuries in some form of suspended animation, to awaken when the malfunction occurs. But the basic story would be the same as the actual event—the mission, the malfunction, the correction (or noncorrection) of the malfunction, the safe return or continuance of the voyage.

Soft S.F.

The changes might be the same as for the hard s.f. example. However, the story might revolve more around the relationships among the crew members—human, alien, robot, or a mixture. It might stress the psychological effects on a particular crew member in the spacecraft on his home planet. The malfunction might not be in the spacecraft but of a medical type that affects the crew members. Whatever the malfunction or problem, it would be logically presented, based on scientific cause and solved scientifically, even if the science is theoretical or yet to be discovered.

Fantasy

The malfunction or problem is not solved scientifically. It might involve the use of psychic powers to cure an illness or other type of malfunction or to teleport the crew to safety. The power driving the ship might be the psychic powers of the crew or a disembodied mind or minds installed in the spacecraft or on the home planet. Perhaps this mind might be the item that malfunctions, becoming insane. Perhaps the spacecraft is attacked by a space dragon or some other type of impossible animal. The animal or attack might exist only in the minds of the crew or be the mental image defense of a life form that feels threatened by the spacecraft.

Sword & Sorcery

To alter the actual event to fit this category, you would have to follow the rigid rules that apply. Therefore, somehow the captain or a crew member would have to be taken to a planet by some form of magic. He would then become the hero and follow the usual pattern of this category. The basic story would have very little to do with the plot in this category; rather, it would be used merely to get a hero to a certain location in order to begin the story.

Space Opera

Hard or soft s.f. changes could be made to the basic story. However, there is always a hero, and usually it's the captain. Space opera, being basically adventure, does not need to include rational explanations, as long as they sound scientific—but not too much on the fantasy side. Whatever the situation, it's the hero to the rescue and perhaps a maiden in distress. The captain almost singlehandedly repairs the malfunction, finds the formula to cure the malady, fights off the space dragons (real or imaginary), and outwits the villian. Space opera will usually be rejected by genre magazines unless done humorously, as pastiches or take-offs. Space opera is quite popular in the form of movies, TV programs, and novels.

Speculative Fiction

The true story would be written in a very poetic manner and could use any of the elements of hard or soft s.f. or fantasy, but actually no changes would be necessary. The story might be told from the viewpoint of the three crew members, individually, in very flowery language. It is the style of writing that would make the story speculative fiction—but this is merely a label and not a category. A simple statement—"He wondered if he would ever see home again."—whether made by human or alien might be written like this, especially if alien: "No more to hear the bell trees sighing softly their silver song in the wind; no more to see the crystal spires catch the fire of the dawn; nomorenomoreno-morenomore. . . ."

If flowery enough, this style of writing can so dilute the science that the story no longer seems as if it is science fiction at all.

Mixed-Genre

The actual event is already a mixed-genre—both s.f. and suspense, which is part of the mystery genre: the world waited anxiously during the dangerous return trip. However, it isn't a true mixture, just a bit more suspenseful than most s.f. A more complete mixture might make the malfunction the result of sabotage (a crime) with the attempt to find out "who done it," or perhaps a race against time to find another bit of sabotage (maybe a weakened electrical connection), before it can short out and kill the crew. Any of the hard or soft s.f. changes could also be made and still keep the mystery/s.f. mixture.

Horror

One of the crew members is killed messily in the malfunction. The other crew members keep seeing him in all of his gory form walking (or floating) among them. Or hear his voice. Or perhaps the crew sees hideous shapes in or outside the spacecraft. The crew might be haunted by the ghosts of the astronauts who perished in the fire or by alien space travelers that appear as ghosts. Or something alien might be in the spacecraft, waiting to seize an unwary crewman.

Alternate History

This category is the most difficult to apply to the basic story. A bit of history, altered at a certain point in time, might result in the crew members not being from the United States for any of a number of reasons, mainly because the country failed to come into existence. But this would be only a very minor change, and any of the other category changes could be made.

Pivoting this plot on the alternate-history device would not really affect the story structure; it would remain about the same.

You will note that none of these examples represents a single, pure example of each category. Most stories do contain such a mixture, but the emphasis is usually on one category.

2

Science Fiction Reading Sources

If you don't *read* science fiction or fantasy, don't attempt to write it. The written form of the genre is vastly different from what is presented in its dramatic forms. Written s.f. constantly evolves, and new concepts are continually being published. Dramatic, or performed, s.f. is very expensive to produce. It is done for entertainment and profit and is geared toward the general public (not the s.f. community), because that's where the profit is. Therefore, dramatic s.f. specializes in tried-and-true formulas, even if the movie or TV show is based on an s.f. book or story and/or written by an s.f. writer. Numerous people are involved with the production—people who are not part of the science fiction world—and this will alter the final product. What makes the current crop of s.f. movies and TV shows different from the pre–*Star Wars* presentations is the use of new techniques and improved technology to create spectacular special effects, as well as depiction of space technology that is more complex and realistic, based on what we know today.

If you use the definitions and examples presented in this book, you will at once realize that *Star Wars* used a hard s.f. background but was basically space opera with a bit of sword and sorcery. But you would have to own a videorecorder and a cassette of a highly successful s.f. film for any movie to be of use to you as a writer. You would have to examine it moment by moment and have the written script in front of you at the same time. Only then would you discover any flaws in logic and science as well as in dialogue, which is the "writing" in a visual presentation.

A book or story can be read bit by bit; you can go over sentences and paragraphs, rereading them and comparing one type of story or novel to another. Only in the written genre will you be able to judge just what is being bought by editors and recognize changes in trends in s.f. themes, concepts, and techniques and styles of writing, as well as in categories. For all of these reasons, you must read current s.f.

The best way to keep up with the huge output of current s.f. and fantasy is to read, along with other s.f. literature, the three highly regarded monthly s.f. magazines. These appear at newsstands (and can be subscribed to) and contain more fiction than the other magazines: *Analog Science Fiction/Science Fact* ("Analog"), *The Magazine of Fantasy & Science Fiction* ("F&SF"), and *Isaac Asimov's Science Fiction Magazine* ("IASFM"). You will then be reading approximately two dozen stories each month—a combination of short-short and short stories, novellas, novelettes, and book serializations.

The greatest number of monthly horror stories are to be found in *Rod Serling's The Twilight Zone Magazine.*

These magazines also contain other items of interest to prospective s.f. writers, such as articles (primarily about science and technology), s.f. book and/or drama reviews, convention information, and letters.

Then there are original anthologies, including the continuing series anthologies, and, of course, the latest novels.

It is advisable that you read the fiction of the past as well. Starting with the present year, work backward for a few decades. As you go further into the past writings, you will see reflected in the fiction the different themes and concepts of the story lines prevalent at the time in which they were published. They will also reflect the society of that particular time, because that social structure was integrated into the framework of the story. You will see themes and concepts much used for a while and then discarded, perhaps because of new scientific advances or new directions in writing style.

For shorter works, reprint anthologies and collections (works by a single writer) are always being published, as well as reprints (mainly paperbacks) of novels. You can find a large selection of older material in the library.

Science Source Materials

Reading science fiction is not enough.

Many s.f. writers, and readers as well, have science or technical backgrounds, having degrees noted after their names such as Ph.D., M.D., and others. Many simultaneously work in these sciences or professions and write s.f. And their stories reflect these backgrounds.

But what of the s.f. writers who do not have any higher (college) education in any science, whose stories appear to indicate scientific knowledge? These writers have done their homework and know at least the basics of their subject matter. They have read the necessary nonfiction in order to write this fiction.

What science source materials are best for s.f. writers?

If you have any scientific background, you may be able to understand the more technical articles, papers, and magazines, but usually only in your particular area. An astrophysicist might not be able to comprehend fully a highly technical paper on the latest medical advance in gene splicing, nor would an attorney be likely to follow the complicated set of mathematics of a new theory on the origin of earthquakes. But they could understand a more popularized version of the same subjects. A number of general science magazines, such as *Science Digest, Science 82* (the number changes to reflect each year), and *Discovery,* have articles on the latest advances, discoveries, and theories; they are written for the general public and are therefore easy to understand. *Scientific American* is another excellent source, but it presents information more technically than the others and is therefore for the more scientifically oriented.

There are magazines devoted to specific subjects, such as astronomy, psychology, computers, and technology. There are medical and legal publications that can be understood by a more educated general public. And the magazines written for s.f. readers, such as *Omni* and the other s.f. genre magazines, have informative articles. New discoveries are usually reported by the wire services and appear in newspapers and the news magazines. *The New York Times* has a special science section every Tuesday. Books on general science subjects and specific topics are constantly being published.

What about other nonfiction?

In science fiction, imagination is unlimited. Ideas can be sparked by any subject, and most likely some factual material that the general public can understand is written about that subject. Any nonfiction subject is apt to be a source of material.

3
Ideas

Generating Ideas

How do you get ideas?

One of the most basic methods is to extrapolate—from any source, any subject matter. In doing so, apply the three *ifs* of science fiction:

1. What if . . . ?
2. If only . . . .
3. If this goes on . . . .

By applying any or all of these *ifs* to any subject, an idea should be generated. For example, assume you are watching a TV newscast. Part of this program is devoted to sports, and the headline topic is a baseball strike. To fill the time slot and placate the many baseball fans, the station shows a few highlights from a major league ball game—but from exactly one year before. How can you apply the three *ifs* to this scenario?

What if for any reason there was no general news of any kind for a period of time (at least a day or so), and the station rebroadcast the news of the day from the date of exactly one year before?

If only you could watch some of the great baseball games in their entirety that were played before anyone thought to record them on TV tape or film—maybe a game from the beginning of the twentieth century?

If this goes on, will it be the end of professional major league baseball? Will a new summertime sport be invented to fill the sports gap? What will this future be like?

These examples do not entail any particular hard science or any soft science, other than the human experience. Now, to extrapolate further, ask yourself: What would cause the problem in "What if"? How could you watch the past in "If only"? And what is the future and future sport in "If this goes on"? These examples are nonscience general-topic extrapolations.

What of a mixture of scientific and general subjects?

You are reading an article about an investigation into the possible causes of senility in the aged and a probable method of halting or even helping to reverse certain symptoms and effects of senility. You might start to think about people being able to live much longer than they do now—perhaps for centuries— without the debilitating effects of senility or aging in general. What effect would that have on society? What would this world be like? Where and how would people live? You may think that this theme has been done before and you would have nothing new to say—and file these thoughts away. Then, as you are reading this book—in particular, the section on copyright—your prior thoughts might return, and now you find you have a new idea to go with the theme of longevity. How would this affect the life-plus-fifty-years length of copyright? *What if* a life span were five hundred years?

And then you remember reading articles on cryogenics.

What if a writer, who had been put into a state of suspended animation through freezing, was thawed several hundred years later? Thanks to medical advancement that took place during his "sleep," he can now live many centuries. And upon his return to consciousness, he learns that he now has the same respect and esteem as Shakespeare has today. *What if* he demands that his copyrights be returned to him since he is no longer dead?

What of an extrapolation on a personal experience?

For example, you live in a major city where there is rent control. Due to an addition to the family, you need a larger apartment, but none are available. They are all rent-controlled and occupied by elderly widows who, due to their dire financial straits and the low rental of their too large apartments, cannot afford to move, though they would very much like to.

If this goes on, who would be able to have children?

If only there were some way to get rid of these old women.

What if murder were legalized?

What sort of future society would legalize murder, under what conditions? How would anyone literally get a "license to kill"? Would all the red tape that is necessary today to apply for anything governmental be even worse when transported to this future? You now have a mixed-genre idea.

What of a combination of nonfiction and fiction, otherwise known as an ad?

For example, you notice an automobile ad in a magazine that implies that the items normally included in an automobile are "extras," given free with a particular car.

What if a couple of glib auto salesmen were determined to con what they considered a stupid cash-sale prospect into paying for "extras" that were really part of the new car and that customer didn't want the engine because he had a much better gadget with which to replace the engine? You now have the beginning of a humorous s.f. story.

Relax. Let your imagination run free. In the s.f. genre there are no boundaries to original thought.

As soon as you have a substantial idea, write it down in a few brief sentences so that you can develop it more fully. If you are not able to begin writing your story immediately, file this idea description in a special folder to keep your thoughts from being lost. You may want to consult the other ideas in this folder before writing any story.

Idea Development: Building Your Universe

Themes and Concepts

In science fiction and fantasy, certain ideas in plots are used over and over again. These ideas are referred to within the genre as themes and/or concepts.

Themes that have been often used and accepted before do not have to be explained in any great detail. Sometimes explanations are eliminated entirely, the assumption being that the reader is familiar with the theme. However, you might have an unusually original idea (or concept) of that theme, which would have to be explained.

A few of the many themes and/or concepts are utopias, dystopias, time travel, parallel universes (or worlds), alternate universes (or worlds), galactic empires, clones, faster-than-light travel, intelligent life forms (also called extraterrestrials or aliens), ESP, psychic powers, and terraforming. One recently popular fantasy theme is dragons—with or without flame throwing, grounded or flying. You don't have to explain the dragons in great detail to have them accepted as a necessary part of your story. But, suppose a character in your story built and used a mechanical flying dragon? That would be a new concept (idea) within a theme and would definitely have to be explained. Galactic empires are definite themes, and one day these themes may become a category, but each writer using this general theme has a different version of a galactic empire. This difference lies in the history, inhabitants, etc., of the concept (idea) of each galactic empire. Asimov's "three laws of robotics" is a concept of the logical method for controlling robots and is so well known that a writer may merely refer to the "first law," and not only have no need to write it out but may never even explain it.

Plotting

Themes and/or concepts are not stories; they are merely components of a story. If you mistake these for the plot itself, you will get nothing for your efforts but rejection slips. You must tell a story.

Stories are stories in any genre—they have a beginning, a middle, and an end. They contain characters of some sort; even robots and intelligent bacteria can be considered characters. There is at least one protagonist. There are obstacles to be overcome. The action takes place in a particular setting, but the setting itself should not be considered more important than the action of the story. And the characters should be given depth and not be cardboard or two-dimensional.

Let's use a story possibility discussed earlier and develop it further.

It might be easiest to start with a definite protagonist possibility—the thawed writer. The basic idea is close to a complete plot, but a lot is missing. It might be best to start the story just after his being thawed and before he awakens. Then you could have several characters discuss the writer's past, why he was frozen, their awe at defrosting such a legendary writer. This would take care of explaining the writer's background. Now your actual detailed plotting could begin.

Suppose you conceive of this story as being long, perhaps as long as a novel. You would then need secondary plots running through the story, apart from the basic plot—the writer's attempt to regain his copyrights. More characters would be needed, and they would have to be developed with more depth.

But perhaps you want this story to be much shorter, no more than 5,000 words. If so, you would quickly have to get to the basic problem and resolve it. No matter what the story length, you would still have to depict the society into which the writer awakens. The shorter the story, however, the less wordage available for this.

Your basic plot, keeping the story short, might be: writer awakens; learns of the events that have occurred while he was frozen; is astounded to discover his renown; goes off to live in the world on his own; needs funds; discovers that he can't write, perhaps because the society of the present is too different from that of the past, because there are other thawed celebrities and he isn't unique enough to make money lecturing or appearing on what would be the entertainment media (something akin to TV, but advanced); remembers the terms of his copyrights when he sees a reprint of one of his books, for which he does not get paid; retains a lawyer and files a suit against the government and publishers for his rights under the copyright law; he's the first thawed person to do this; and then . . .

The story has to be resolved in some manner. Some struggle has to be depicted, perhaps the trial of the suit. But you may not know very much about legal matters, so it would be entirely too difficult to fictionalize any legal proceedings.

So, if showing the action of the trial is impossible for you, you might have the writer and his lawyers discussing this action or show it in some other manner. And what ending do you want? Does the writer win, lose, or is his problem resolved in an entirely different manner? You cannot resolve the problem through the introduction of any gadget that does not appear elsewhere in the story, such as some sort of time machine to whisk him back to his own past. The resolution has to come from within the framework of the story and its theme/concept.

Getting the Science Right

On the surface, the above plot may not seem to contain any science, but it does. You are going to have a human being who has been frozen and thawed—brought back to life, so to speak. No matter how briefly you may depict this, there are certain anatomical, biological, and other physiological events that occur—and you've got to get them right.

A person who has not moved a particular joint or muscle for even a few weeks (such as when encased in a cast because of a broken bone) cannot bend that joint or use that muscle. After several months flat on your back with your leg held firmly in traction due to a broken hip, your knee joint will be "locked" and you will find it difficult to sit up due to weakened back muscles.

So just imagine what effect several centuries of inaction will do to a body. The person would be completely helpless, unable to move anything, unable even to open his eyes, swallow, or breathe on his own. You may assume that somehow medical science will find a way to activate all functions—even mental functions—of a body. But the thawed person would still be very weak, far more frail than a newborn baby who would have had a good deal of exercise in the womb. It would be illogical to depict in a scene a frozen person who is thawed in a few minutes, breathes, opens his eyes, asks, "Where am I?", sits up, and walks out of the room.

Movies and TV will do this sort of scene. An s.f. writer, however, should have a bit of common sense, at the very least, and should have done some research on the subject. Your thawed writer is going to need some very extensive physical therapy and rehabilitation, even to the extent of relearning bladder control. How much of this you want to show and in what manner determines whether or not you want a harder s.f. story.

You are creating a future several centuries from now. There are other, more advanced sciences and technology in this plot. Even if only indicated or mentioned briefly, they are: what the methods of transportation are; what sort of word processor a writer would use; where and how people live; what other medical advances have been made; how any of that time's problems have been solved; what kinds of entertainment fields there are and how they are presented; and what the language is and how it has changed.

Although this plot might be basically soft s.f., and you may not wish to make it harder, preferring to emphasize the social aspects and the human experience, it is set in the future and that implies an advancement in science and technology.

A surprising number of s.f. stories will contain very little science or technology. But whenever any particular science or technology has to be explained or its workings described, it should be correct. You cannot cancel the known rules of science without offering a very good and scientifically feasible substitute.

There are a great many gadgets scattered about in s.f. stories.

Most of the time the detailed workings of these objects are not explained—just that they work and what they do, not *how* they work unless absolutely necessary. A character may step into some kind of booth, twirl a few dials, and instantly be transported to another location. The reader will accept the idea of this being possible without your having to explain how and why it is possible.

However, if the setting of your story is on a planet in a double-star system and you describe a sunset, you had better be scientifically correct as to precisely what would be seen, right down to the exact colors of the sky, because it is scientifically possible to accurately predict such a scene. You cannot fake it. You cannot stretch literary license too far. You must stick to what is provable—even in theory.

Incorrect Science in S.F.

There are three types of flaws that cause incorrect science in s.f.:

1. flaws occurring because of discoveries made after the fiction was published;

2. flaws of logic in a theoretical, postulated, or undiscovered science;

3. flaws due to the total disregard of what is known and provable in a science.

Fictional flaws that come into existence following discoveries made subsequent to a manuscript's publication may be embarrassing to a writer, but these story components were at least correct with regard to the scientific knowledge that existed when the story was done. There are many stories depicting the planet Venus as a steaming jungle or watery world. The Venus probes indicated just what that planet was really like. Today, any fiction about Venus would reflect the known facts.

Flaws of logic may not be apparent, and the flawed science might be acceptable.

The example story of the thawed writer has a flaw of logic, but in law, not in science. No matter how long it may take

Congress to act, you can be sure that at some point before the story begins the copyright law will have been changed by an amendment to make allowances for the new scientific advances of an increase life span and the ability of medical science to thaw frozen people. To be logical, the story would have to mention that change, but it is the extent of the change and some loophole in the law that would be the basis of the thawed writer's suit.

While flaws of discovery and logic may be forgiven by the reader through suspended disbelief and become acceptable, flaws that occur because the writer ignores basic scientific facts are inexcusable. You might think that any writer would know the facts of human reproduction and development—even a non-s.f. writer. Yet there are stories of human clones in which the clone is created within a short period of time (a few days) and is a carbon copy of the original—the exact age, appearance, intelligence, personality, etc. Totally ignored in the fact that a clone has to develop in the exact same manner as any fertilized human egg. Even with exactly the same genetic material there would be considerable differences between the clone and the original due to many factors such as environment and education. Most of the stories containing this type of flaw are not written by s.f. writers, nor do they appear in s.f. publications.

Explanations

Somewhere in a science fiction story there comes a point at which the writer has to explain one or more of his ideas—a new concept on an old theme, an invention, a bit of technology. Older s.f. stories sometimes had a character explaining a gizmo to another character in elaborate detail for paragraph after paragraph. This is no longer done. Explanations should be held to a minimum and should fall within the framework of the story. They should be given very gradually, if at all—as a "sugar-coated pill" in which the story is advanced while pertinent facts are disclosed subtly.

Before you start any explanations, ask yourself if it is really a necessary part of the story line. As stated previously in this book, there are themes and/or concepts that are an accepted part of s.f., for which little or no explanation is necessary.

Just imagine you were writing a different type of fiction, perhaps a mainstream story. Would you have someone explain, in great detail, how an automobile worked and how to drive it every time that character got into a car? Would you explain the scientific workings of electricity and the incandescent bulb every time someone turned on a light?

Everything in your story does not have to be explained, just what is necessary to the logic of the plot. The explanations should not interrupt the flow of the story.

Humor in S.F.

Science fiction stories do not have to be serious. Even though humor is difficult to write, it is found in many forms of s.f. A tall tale–s.f. story can often be far more outrageously funny than a mainstream tall tale. There are parodies of scientific papers. Stories are written lightly, to evoke a smile or a belly laugh. There are the punch line puns done as short-shorts, most notably the "Ferdinand Feghoot" series. Devil stories are done in a mainly humorous tenor rather than in one of horror. Even satire is used in s.f. stories.

Many of the light, humorous stories are done in a format of correspondence, such as letters, office memos, etc.

In punch-line puns, that last sentence is all-important, and the entire story is woven around it. This type of story is best done as a short-short.

Being able to write humor will be to your advantage. Genre magazine editors and anthologists need humorous pieces to give their readers relief from the serious stories.

Poetry

Poetry in science fiction follows every rule of poetry, plus those of science fiction. Poems can be in rhyme or blank verse. Some stories are done as poetry rather than as prose. These poems are not epics, but just another way of writing a story. Poetry does not appear very often, but when it does the poem is considered on a par with the stories and articles in the publication. In s.f. magazines there are no poetry departments each month containing cutesy four-line verses, as in the women's slicks.

Besides regular forms of poetry, there is another kind that appears in science fiction—song lyrics. In some s.f., a song is a part of the story, but since only the words can be given, the reader is left to imagine the music. Many of the song lyrics in s.f. stories have been set to music written by various members of the s.f. community, and these are sung regularly at conventions.

In addition to lyrics within stories, they have been written *about* s.f. stories—even novels—and set to music. Of these, the song about "The Lord of the Rings" is one of the most popular within the s.f. community.

Reality

You may write a story that takes place in the future or on another planet or that is entirely about aliens. But since your reader is human, here on Earth, in this era, the story has to be written in the current language. It would be illogical to suppose that the English language as it is spoken now (especially slang phrases) and the meanings given to words will be the same several centuries in the future. But you cannot invent hundreds of words and phrases or give new meanings to words in your story, because the reader would have a very difficult time following the story line. You would need pages of definitions in a novel. A few words or phrases of current usage might be altered to give the flavor of the invented setting. But too much of this should be avoided, especially in anything shorter than a novel, as it interrupts the story flow.

No matter what kind of society you depict in your story, you will still have a bit of today's social mores in it. This will not be noticeable at the present time. But if your story is published, it will be quite apparent in several decades.

Situations and character types must be identifiable by readers. The overbearing boss or the nagging spouse can be recognized even if that boss is a robot or the spouse is an alien. The anguish of failure and the joy of success will always be the same, regardless of the planet, the time, and the characters to whom these situations may occur.

4
Writing Tips

There are other factors to consider in writing science fiction besides the ones mentioned so far.

It is best to start writing a story after it has been worked out thoroughly—in your mind, in a brief outline, or, if a novel, in even greater detail. While some writers may be able to start a story by setting down a clever opening sentence and continuing from there, this does not always result in a good story.

Use your own ideas. Although there are trends in the use of certain subjects, and you may be inspired by the works of other s.f. writers and tempted to extrapolate on their works, there is a vast abundance of other sources to use as the starting point for your ideas.

Triteness

Avoid being trite in your ideas as well as in your writing. One form of triteness is the use of "surprise" endings; for example, depicting an archaeological expedition on a planet and then having one of your characters announce at the end of the story, "So this was the planet Earth!" after leading the reader to believe that the action took place elsewhere. There are a lot of variations on this type of ending in many beginning writers' stories: the Garden of Eden as the setting, the characters being aliens instead of human, or the protagonist revealed as God. The scientists in s.f. stories are not "mad" scientists as depicted in old Grade B movies, and aliens do not exist merely to conquer Earth or terrorize humans.

Then there is triteness in writing such as revealing certain facts that the reader must know. The sample story of the thawed writer could contain just such a defect by having two characters discuss the background of the writer at the very beginning of the story, instead of releasing this information more gradually throughout the first part of the text.

Dialogue and Action

Try to write dialogue that will follow speech patterns and word usages as if they were to be spoken aloud instead of being read silently. Printed conversation is different from oral, because people (or any other beings) will not speak so smoothly or fluently, so a writer should try to strike a balance between what looks good and what will sound good.

Show the action in a story, instead of having your characters discuss it. It is far more dramatic to depict a scene in which a disaster occurs—such as an astronaut working outside his spacecraft and suddenly becoming detached and floating away into space—than to have one character say to another, "Hey, did you hear what happened to Charlie?" Such a scene would merely be tediously dragged out while one character asked questions and the other gave answers.

Other Points

Don't clutter your story with unnecessary details or too many intricately involved technical descriptions or explanations. A reader will accept the fact that your character is wearing a shimmering dress that glows and changes colors according to her mood. If the dress has nothing to do with the plot, you don't have to explain the complete history of this invention, what the material is composed of, how it was manufactured, how it works, or other scientifically related facts.

Keep the focus of your story consistent. If your story line is about a thawed writer trying to regain his copyright, you cannot suddenly push him into the background and make his lawyer the main character in the second half of the story.

If at all possible, tell the story in the sequence in which it happens. Flashbacks can sometimes interrupt story flow.

If you plan to have your story run to 5,000 words, and it won't go more than 3,000, end it there. Don't try to pad. On the other hand, don't try to cram into a short story material that should be in a novel.

An Education in Writing

There are many courses available on the techniques of writing general fiction. And numerous courses specifically address science fiction, both for the understanding and appreciation of the literature and for instruction on how to write in the genre. Certain of these courses are taught in colleges and universities in regular academic programs. You could, no doubt, enroll in your area for a class or two a week without taking credits. You might take classes that are sometimes conducted at night. Also, evening courses for adults are given in high schools by local boards of education. Sometimes the instructors of these courses are well-known s.f. writers.

There are also conferences and workshops specializing exclusively in science fiction; these are given in various locations in the United States and elsewhere. They are advertised primarily in the s.f. genre magazines and newszines. Most of these conferences and workshops have a limited enrollment. Some of them can last for over a month; others can run for from a few days to a week or two.

One of the oldest is the Milford Science Fiction Writers'

Conference, which was created for professional writers, with attendance by invitation only. It was from the group associated with this conference that the Science Fiction Writers of America (SFWA) was formed.

The best-known open workshop is the Clarion Science Fiction Workshop, now held at Michigan State University in East Lansing. Clarion is one of the longer workshops, lasting six weeks. There are a number of big-name writers in residence. The students, beginning and aspiring writers, pay a fee ($1,000 or more, but the fee is less for Michigan residents) to cover their stay in the dormitories. And, during this time they write. Morning sessions are presided over by one of the resident writers, with a limited number of students in each class. The stories are passed around and criticized by all of the students and then the resident writer. Finally the author of the work is given an opportunity to speak about it. This procedure is followed every day for the entire six weeks. A number of Clarion graduates have become well-known writers.

Not all workshops and conferences are run in the same manner as Clarion.

Sometimes, in order to qualify to attend a workshop or conference, the applicant is required to submit a manuscript of a given length. If the applicant is accepted, the work is critiqued by the resident writers.

The shorter conferences and workshops are, of course, much less expensive to attend and are very intensive, cramming a lot into a short time—a few days to a week.

But at any of these conferences and workshops there is one quality you must possess—you have to be able to accept criticism and realize that it is not directed at you personally but only at your fiction, even though most writers consider their work an extension of themselves.

There are other general writing workshops and conferences, advertised primarily in the general writers' magazines, *Writer's Digest* and *The Writer*.

But it is not really necessary to take any formal courses or attend a workshop or conference to learn how to write or how to write science fiction. Many available books, written by well-known and experienced writers, might help you. Many of these books illustrate, step by step, how that particular author wrote a story, showing where the ideas came from, how they were developed, and the style of writing and storytelling used. This can be quite helpful if you encounter similar situations in your writing. Then there are some books with each chapter written by a different author, giving opinions and suggestions for writing fiction in general, or s.f. specifically, and also showing how certain writing problems are solved. This can be a very interesting look into the thoughts of various writers and their methods of writing.

When selecting books on writing, be certain to choose those that provide you with good, substantial information on the craft.

There are certain books on writing and selling any type of fiction (or nonfiction) that do not really tell you how to write or sell—just what to do and how to run your career *after* you are an established and well-known writer.

Again, most particularly, you must *read* science fiction.

Collaborations

In science fiction, you create your own universe and you and your collaborator would have to reach an agreement on each and every detailed aspect of the story, in addition to the style of writing. This task is difficult enough in other types of fiction, but unbelievably difficult in science fiction.

In the process of collaboration, your ideas may be discarded or so altered that you no longer recognize them.

You may indeed find a compatible writer with whom to collaborate on a story from its very inception, but this is rare. Most of the collaborations that are published are written by well-known and experienced writers.

Of course, if you have a completed manuscript and an experienced and well-known writer offers to help you in order to make the manuscript salable by collaborating with you, it would be foolish to refuse such an offer. Please note, however, that in such cases the manuscript should be completed before collaboration begins; it is best to have all of your thoughts down on paper before attempting to share them with anyone else.

General Fiction—Writers' Trade Magazines and Books

In addition to the s.f. genre newszines with their wealth of material for writers (see Publications, Chapter 10), there are writers' magazines which are devoted to writing in general, both fact and fiction. Occasionally they publish an article written by a well-known s.f. writer regarding some phase of science fiction or fantasy writing. A number of articles appear in each monthly issue, written by established writers, telling of their experiences in writing and giving helpful tips on various aspects of writing in general, sometimes on the writing of s.f. and other genres. Each month there are listings of specific subject markets, usually just for the magazines. Sometimes the book markets are included in this type of subject listing. These magazines try to keep up with what is happening in the whole writing trade.

There are writers' reference books, published on a yearly basis, listing all writing categories. These books provide writing and marketing tips, as well as market information on magazines, including specialized and trade magazines, and on books. The names and addresses of publishers are listed, including editors (if applicable), their needs including the titles of books they've recently published, payment rates and royalty percentages, and other useful facts.

The magazines are available at most libraries or can be obtained at newsstands and by subscription from the publishers.

Writer's Digest	The Writer
9933 Alliance Rd.	8 Arlington St.
Cincinnati, OH 45242	Boston, MA 02116

Writer's Digest also publishes *Writer's Yearbook,* an annual magazine, the annual *Writer's Market,* and *Writers' and Artists' Yearbook,* which is edited in England and lists international markets. *The Writer* annually publishes *The Writer's Handbook.*

Literary Market Place (LMP), another annual publication, contains a wide range of information, including listings of book and magazine publishers, agents, grants, literary awards, and writers' organizations and conferences. It is published by:

> R. R. Bowker Co.
> 1180 Avenue of the Americas
> New York, NY 10036

These annuals are available at most libraries or can be obtained from bookstores or from the publishers.

Writers' Reference Books

As general tools of the trade, you should have a good unabridged dictionary. Also get a thesaurus: *Roget's International Thesaurus*, Crowell, Fourth Edition, is the largest, most comprehensive book of its kind. You should also have a book on grammar and usage.

A general science book or encyclopedia is also useful. The essays of Asimov, originally published in *F&SF,* are reprinted in several collections. These are very informative and easy to understand by the general public.

These reference books should be at hand for easy reference when you write.

PART II: THE SCIENCE FICTION COMMUNITY

Just as the academe discovered s.f. literature, some day the sociologists will discover the s.f. community. And when they do, they will have a wealth of material to investigate.

The s.f. community is far more than just fans and pros. It is comprised of the people interested in science fiction in a community of worldwide proportion. It is not a cult or subculture, though there are various groups within the community. It is a society whose members are involved in s.f. activities in their own countries and who communicate through literature, fanzines, letters, meetings, and conventions with other groups in this international network.

The Value of the S.F. Community

There are readers of s.f. genre fiction who call themselves fans but who are not active within the community. On the other hand, there are readers who are also devoted to s.f. (and fantasy) who know nothing about the community. Through the s.f. genre magazines, with their publication of letters and listings of conventions, these s.f. readers and enthusiasts—a constantly growing population of the "uninitiated" (as they are called by the fans)—are regularly informed of the doings of the community and cons, whetting their appetites to join the ranks of convention goers.

Publishers who are in the s.f. community know its value. Any publisher or editor who seriously wants to enter the field should become part of the community. Both writers and the fans like to meet with them. This personal contact is very important to the community.

The informal atmosphere and ease with which publishers can engage in conversation with many available writers—both established and new—and even in group discussions, sparks ideas and friendships that can lead to future contracts to the advantage of all concerned. Many anthologies and other s.f. projects have been conceived and followed through as a result of just these conditions. And it also provides an opportunity for publishing people to learn of the latest trends of interest among the reading fans of the genre.

Publishers take special suites at the major cons, especially at the Worldcon, as does SFWA. They display their latest releases, appear on con programs, and advertise in the newszines and s.f. genre magazines.

If a book publisher really wants to push a writer, it will advertise outside the genre, in newspapers, sometimes without labeling the novel as s.f.; other times it is to their advantage to label the work.

The publishers and editors have an opportunity, through the conventions, fanzines, and newszines, to be in contact with those who purchase their releases—their products. They can readily tell which writer is popular, whose fiction is highly regarded (especially important to a beginning writer), and what the fans want in reading material. The s.f. community gives editors and publishers a direct means of informing a large number of aspiring writers, as well as the more experienced, of their needs and tastes in s.f. and fantasy through personal contact, by appearing on con programs, and by giving tips to the newszines.

Besides the informal contacts with editors and publishers at s.f. conventions, writers are admired by the fans (a very heady experience for a writer) and thus have contact with their readers. By appearing at cons, being on programs, and being visible, a writer can gain a large following of fans who will look for his fiction and buy it. And if that fiction is good enough, and a writer has a large following, he can even win awards. The vast number of readers of s.f. are outside the community, and new people are continuously discovering s.f.

The winning of an award is subsequently capitalized on thereafter whenever a writer's fiction appears—on the covers of genre magazines, on dust jackets of all books, and in ads— "A New Story by the Hugo (or Nebula) Award–Winning Author!"—hopefully to generate more sales.

Aspiring writers get a chance to listen to and speak with these editors, publishers, and established writers at conventions, as well as at seminars, conferences, and workshops. And they get the very latest market information through the newszines.

The numerous bookstores that have opened in the last few years that specialize in science fiction are another result of burgeoning fandom and the ever-growing s.f. community. The readers have a specialized store at which to purchase their favorite reading material. And these stores serve as a gathering place for fans, readers, and writers. A publisher (or perhaps the writer) will arrange to have autograph sessions at these s.f. bookstores whenever a new book is released or sometimes whenever a writer is in town. Because of the commercial success of these bookstores specializing in s.f., and the popularity of the autograph sessions, regular (general) bookstores and bookstore chains are now also holding these autograph sessions with s.f. writers—and advertising these events in the newspapers. All of this activity generates more sales, both for the writer whose work is featured and for all s.f. works in general.

5

The Fans

The Origin of Fandom

How did this community begin?

With its literature. Modern s.f., as opposed to classical s.f.—
Wells, Verne, etc.—arose in the United States in the 1920s, when
the first pulp s.f. magazines appeared. This early s.f. consisted
primarily of stories. Compared to the number of novels issued
each year today, few were published in the early days.

The readers of those magazines wrote letters, which were
published in the magazines. They got together, formed local
clubs, and issued amateur publications known as *fanzines*. Clubs
began to meet with other clubs. This was the beginning of
fandom. Those who were the early fans, up until 1938, are
referred to collectively as *First Fandom*.

In 1939 the first World Science Fiction Convention (Nycon)
was held in New York City and, except for three years during
World War II, the World S.F. Convention has since been held
annually.

41

Fans were not just the readers, but the writers as well. Some fans later became writers. And writers, as well as editors, became fans. The writers were the "pros," and the pros were the elite. "Fans" came to mean only the readers, and the term *pros* was applied to anyone involved with the professional part of science fiction. As the genre grew beyond the literature itself, the pros began to include artists and those involved in the entertainment fields: the writers and producers of movies, radio, stage, and TV.

The early fans were interested in science and technology, as well as s.f. literature. Today, there are fans who are merely interested in fandom itself—the conventions, the club meetings, and other fannish activities—rather than in reading s.f.

Fans enjoy getting together. As a result, the s.f. community has many conventions. And you, as an aspiring writer, can benefit from this.

It Can Happen to You

What is your favorite daydream of yourself as a writer?

Perhaps you may imagine that a big-name writer will call you to say that he has just signed a contract for an original anthology and just has to have a story from you. You might fantasize that you enter a room with many people, including a big-name or even superstar writer who greets you like a long lost friend. Then he walks you over to an editor or publisher and introduces you as an up-and-coming writer.

Impossible?

Not in the world of science fiction—the real world of the s.f. community.

Because it can be who you know that counts.

And in science fiction, if you join the community, you can meet a lot of "whos."

Yes, editors do publish first works by s.f. writers whom they have never met, whose work came in unsolicited. And in the end the fiction always must speak for itself. For a beginning writer, no amount of influence works if the story is not right for publication.

But how very much easier it is to get that first reading when the editor knows you and can be addressed by you on a first-name basis! It is encouraging to know that your manuscript will not end up on the slush pile but will be read immediately upon receipt—and by the top editor, not a first reader. How nice it is to be able to get an opinion of your manuscript from a well-known professional writer, whom you know will be glad to help you. What an opportunity for an aspiring writer to sit in a room with established writers and listen to their discussions about their works, experiences, and the profession in general. What better education in writing than to have an established writer give you requested advice on any aspect of the profession of writing.

The Social Structure

To a fan, the writers are the elite. Yet, the writers have entirely different criteria for choosing their elite. To a writer, the people who purchase the manuscripts are at the top of the ladder. Therefore the publishers; editors; movie, TV, radio, and stage producers are the elite to any writer.

The ranking of writers varies with their fame. At the top are the superstars—those writers so famous that their names are known outside the s.f. genre. Next come the big-name writers—those famous only within the s.f. genre. All the rest of the published writers are last in rank. The writers, of course, are usually active or affiliate members of the SFWA or members of other (foreign) s.f. writers' organizations. Then there are the Science Fiction Research Association (SFRA) members (see p. 49) and semiprofessional people—those who publish and whose work appears in fanzines that pay for writing and art. After these are the big-name fans, the well-known fans, and the thousands of rank and file fans.

The Typical Fan

All admirers of s.f., especially those of the literature, are fans, but as the term is used within the community, the fans are usually the active people who meet and/or go to conventions.

Fans are generally of above-average intelligence, primarily young, and a more or less even mixture of male and female. A number of fans have degrees in a science, or their work is connected with some form of science or technology.

For the most part they are interested in all branches and forms of science fiction, but mainly the literature. A fan, because of an enormous amount of science fiction reading, will feel free to offer opinions and criticisms by writing letters to magazines and letters to and articles for fanzines and in discussions at meetings.

Many fans try to keep a collection of all the magazines and books they have read. Some of the collections are unbelievably large and quite valuable. After the death of one such fan, his collection was accepted by a large university.

But the literature is not the only part of s.f. that interests fans. There are admirers of s.f. art as well as literature, and many of the readers also collect paintings and other artwork. Some fans are interested only in the art. A professional s.f. artist is one whose work appears in and on professional magazines and books and on such items as posters and illustrations for movies. They have their own pro organization: the Association of SF Artists (ASFA). All other artists are considered "amateur" or fan artists. Many of these talented fan artists have become professionals. Fans also create jewelry and other artistic objects, which they sell at meetings and conventions.

While most of the fan clubs are formed because of the s.f. literature, there are fans and clubs interested in the other aspects of s.f.

The best known of these other groups are the "Trekkies"—the fans of the TV series "Star Trek." The Trekkies are a very large group, but not all Trekkies are s.f. fans or members of the s.f. community. Trekkies are almost a cult. "Star Trek" (the TV series) was much admired by the fans, and its original adherents were part of the s.f. community. Then they started to hold their own conventions, apart from the regular s.f. conventions, and these special conventions were devoted only to the people and items relating to the TV series—not any other part of s.f. The Trekkies have their own social structure. At the top are the producer and actors in the series (Mr. Spock is quite popular), then the writers of the series, the semipros, big-name fans, and fans.

Then there are fans interested primarily in s.f. poetry. The Science Fiction Poetry Association (SFPA) has been formed, and it gives an annual award, the Rhysling Award (see p. 64).

There are fans devoted entirely to fantasy. They also have their own conventions and give several of their own annual awards. One reason fantasy is still part of science fiction and not entirely a separate genre is that these fantasy fans are part of the s.f. community.

For those fans of the s.f. movies, there is the Academy of Science Fiction, Fantasy & Horror Films. Those who live in or near Los Angeles are especially fortunate, as members can see free screenings of current movies. This academy gives annual awards, and the recent award ceremonies were telecast.

There are comic book and comic strip fans, and they give the comic conventions.

And then there are fans who are interested only in the fandom itself, not science fiction. Some of these people are the spouses, children, or friends of fans. Others join because they have heard of fandom and like its social whirl.

Fandom, and thus the s.f. community, is worldwide today. For many years, special funds have been collected for use in the exchange of fans between North America and other parts of the world: the Trans-Atlantic Fan Fund (TAFF) and the Down-Under Fan Fund (DUFF). These fans are elected by the funds' fan contributors. Fans in other countries hold their own conventions, which any fan or pro can attend, and give their own annual awards—usually to writers of that country only. These fans also attend major conventions held in their part of the world, especially the Worldcon held in North America. There are fans (and thus, conventions) in many countries. To name a few:

Canada, England, Australia, New Zealand, France, Japan, the Netherlands, West Germany, the Scandinavian countries, and Israel.

But for a writer in North America, it is the s.f. community here that is most important. The coveted annual Hugo Awards are given at the Worldcons held here, as are the vast majority of conventions. And it is at these conventions that the writers, as well as the publishers and editors, meet.

6

The Pros

The pros are the many people on the professional side of science fiction. Since this book is about the literature, you will want to know about those professionals.

Publishers, Editors, and Writers

Publishers and editors attend the major conventions because they can meet the writers there and deal with them on a more informal basis than at their offices. They also participate in convention panels or listen to them along with the rest of the audience. They are friendly and approachable.

Many of the editors are young and female, especially the book editors. Some of the editors come from the ranks of the fans, starting out as first readers or assistants and gradually working up to becoming editors, the rationale being that since the fans read so very much and have an in-depth understanding of quality s.f., they are qualified to read the slush pile. Some editors and publishers are also writers or were agents.

The writers are, of course, members of SFWA. So are some of the editors and other qualified professionals.

While everyone knows their social standing within the community, they rarely "pull rank." The members are on a first-name (or nickname) basis with each other. Even a young, new fan can approach Asimov, calling him Isaac, and state opinions on the writer's work or converse on other subjects.

Most of the writers are male, and a good number of them are over age forty. However, there are always new writers coming into the community, most of them young—and more and more female writers are into s.f.

The SFWA members are pleased to welcome new members. The new members seem to cluster together in small groups and form friendships, and these groups all seem to become big names at about the same time. When one friend gets ahead in the field, such as by editing an anthology, this writer brings friends along by buying their stories first, or putting them onto deals that the writer has heard about.

Writers also do blurbs for their friends' books.

The past and present officers and committee members of SFWA are all big names, usually because of the quality of their fiction but sometimes just because they are visible within the community and thus popular.

There are some s.f. writers who long to be mainstream writers. They consider themselves imprisoned in a ghetto of science fiction. Some talk, and even write, about leaving the ghetto and never writing s.f. again—but they don't. The attraction of the genre is so great that it overrides any intentions of defection, and the writers return to writing s.f.

While the writers meet primarily at conventions, they also have the annual Nebula Award weekend, which is primarily for SFWA members and those from the publishing industry. They also get together if they happen to live near each other or travel to New York City to visit publishers, editors, and agents. Writers keep in touch through phone calls and correspondence—especially their correspondence in the *SFWA Forum*.

All is not sweetness and light, however. There are many

violent disagreements on what are considered SFWA matters. And there are personality clashes and cliques within the organization. But, basically, the writers are friendly and would be glad to help an aspiring writer.

The Academe

Certain members of the academe, while not usually lumped with the professionals, are also affiliate or institutional members of SFWA and thus a part of the s.f. community. The academe has its own organization, the Science Fiction Research Association (SFRA), founded in 1970. SFRA administers the Jupiter Awards and gives its own award, the Pilgrim. The academe publishes large amounts of scholarly nonfiction regarding aspects of science fiction and a periodical, *Extrapolation*, and holds its own conferences.

Many s.f. writers also teach science fiction—usually the writing of the genre—in colleges, universities, and adult (extension) courses, as well as at workshops and conferences. Thus some writers are also members of the academe.

7

The Conventions

The fans have an acronym, *fiawol*—fandom is a way of life.

Fans love to get together, and their special way of life is nowhere more apparent than at conventions.

Conventions are held worldwide, in countries that have organized fan groups. There are at least 100 conventions per year, and the majority of "cons" (as conventions are called) are held in the United States.

There are yearly conventions sponsored by fan groups in their cities or in the immediate vicinity. For example, the Philadelphia group puts on Philcon; the Lunarians (a New York/New Jersey group) sponsor Lunacon; Disclave is the con sponsored by the Washington, DC, group; Kubla Khan is in Nashville; Westercon is in Phoenix; and Norwescon is held in Seattle. Conventions are held in and around most major cities and a few smaller ones and in nearly every state.

The largest of the cons is Worldcon, which is bid for (two years in advance of the actual date) by fan groups anywhere in the world. Primarily, this convention has been held in English-speaking countries, mostly in the United States. Thus the site of the Worldcon changes from year to year. This particular convention is always held over Labor Day Weekend.

There are one-time conventions, which are the smaller cons. Sometimes these are so popular that they eventually become annual events.

Conventions are held in hotels, usually one hotel. However, the Worldcon now attracts so many attendees (thousands) that it has, for the last few years, used several hotels and a convention hall. This tends to dilute the fun of a convention somewhat, since it is difficult to go from room to room (and thus from party to party) when this also means going from hotel to hotel.

Conventions are always held on weekends. There is an attendance fee, varying in amount, but the highest is for the Worldcon, which can run to $50 per person. The fee is lower if you pay in advance than it is at the door. Most of the attendees stay at the hotel for the entire weekend—even those who may live in the convention city—because it is at night, after the regular programs, that the fun begins.

Conventions usually fill the entire hotel. Because these hotels are usually booked solid, it is best to reserve your room in advance. Hotels give special lower rates for attendees.

Since many fans do not have very much money, and cons can be quite expensive, it is an accepted practice for several fans to share a room for a proportionate contribution toward its cost. Some fans are allowed to stay in the con suite, and some fans will allow anyone to share their room without payment. A fan or two may rent an entire suite in order to have large parties and finance it by sharing the sleeping arrangements with other fans. Pros rarely allow this. Usually the pro room sharers are restricted to the beginning writers who also do not have much money.

Fans and pros start to arrive on Friday afternoon. They register with the hotel and with the convention. If you have already paid your attendance fee, you are on a preregistration list and have only to give your name or ticket. Attendees get some form of identification name badge, a program book, and other printed material, such as ballots for activities, last-minute information, ads for other conventions and for books, and huckster information.

There is usually a party sponsored by the convention fan group on Friday night—sometimes at the con suite. Afterward private parties are held in the hotel rooms.

The hucksters' room is not usually opened until Saturday morning, and it remains open until the con closes late Sunday afternoon. The huckster room consists of many tables filled with the wares of fandom: back and current issues of magazines; used books; jewelry; artwork items associated with stories, TV shows, or movies (such as the furry Tribbles from "Star Trek" or masks of aliens); fanzines and news magazines; comic books; s.f. games and game programs; and anything related to science fiction or fantasy. Sometimes there are several rooms of these tables. The huckster room resembles a gigantic indoor flea market devoted entirely to s.f., and you could easily spend an entire day there. If you go, devote at least a few hours to this room, preferably early Saturday morning, because the good items (books) go first and fast.

If a SFWA (pronounced *sef-wah*) meeting is scheduled, it is held either Saturday or Sunday morning, at least an hour before the programs begin. These meetings are for SFWA members only, as they are the business meetings.

Sometimes a con will have programs or an informal "act" (happening) by a writer on Friday night. Occasionally, movies start on Friday night. But for the majority of cons, the programming begins Saturday morning. The larger cons, such as the Worldcon, will have several programs scheduled simultaneously, leaving the attendees to decide which is more to their liking.

One of the program features consists of panel discussions on any number of s.f. topics, sometimes with writers, fans, and those from the publishing industry. Other panel discussions may be held among just editors, writers, or fans. There is always audience participation, usually a question-and-answer session at the end of the more formal panel discussions; however, this interaction can be the entire panel discussion. Sometimes the program includes slide shows or bits of movies.

There are also speeches by various pros—usually including a big-name or superstar writer. Sometimes this is a formal type of speech, but often it could be described as an "act" when the writer is exceptionally theatrical in his presentation. Popular writers often give a reading of their shorter works.

Conventions always have a pro Guest of Honor (GOH), who is usually a writer, and a fan GOH, always a big-name fan. The main GOH is always the pro. The pro GOH's formal speech is either at a banquet (if there is one) on Saturday night and/or on Saturday or Sunday afternoon.

The Saturday programs are usually over by 5:00 p.m., but an "act" can run an hour or more into overtime.

If there is a banquet, you are required to make your reservations in advance. Few tickets are available once the con begins. While the dress for everything else is quite informal—comfort being of utmost importance—banquets are dress-up occasions. But dressing up in the s.f. community is different from that in the outside world. Garb can range from what might be considered normal clothing to that of other eras, such as the Middle Ages (or earlier), the wearing of cloaks (with swords), or even dress that is related to favorite s.f. or fantasy stories.

The awards, if any, are usually presented after the banquets, but lately the Worldcon has merely had a presentation ceremony and no banquet due to the large number of attendees. The awards are given only in connection with special cons—Worldcon, Fool-Con, the World Fantasy Convention, etc. The annual regional cons rarely have any such awards.

After the banquet—if there is one—or at about 9:00 p.m., there is usually a con party at whatever serves the hotel as a smaller ballroom. You have to pay for the drinks, but many of the con attendees are there. It is usually at this larger party that you can find out where the private parties are being held, and you may get several invitations.

Saturday night is when the costume competition is held, usually starting after the con party. Many cons, especially the large ones, have these competitions. Most costumes are home-made, but the quality and craftsmanship are exceptionally spectacular. Hollywood could not do better. Prizes in various categories are usually awarded. At the Worldcon, the costume competition is held immediately after the award ceremonies.

Also running during most of the con are movies. At some cons new movies or old favorites (such as *2001: A Space Odyssey*) are part of the program, as are entire shows from a TV series (such as "Star Trek") or bits of TV shows, such as the outtakes. Most of the movies are the Grade B oldies.

Some cons have electronic and other games, which are quite popular, in special rooms.

In the evenings the fun begins. People go from room to room or stand or sit in hallways, conversing, drinking, munching, laughing, and singing. Room parties always provide something to drink, something to nibble on. An amazing number of people manage to squeeze into a room—and overflow into the halls. Some rooms hold open houses, but usually just to fans or pros who are known to the party giver. One way to be welcomed into a room party is to bring liquid refreshment with you for all to share: beer, soda, or a bottle of something "hard." Some fans manage to pack a guitar, and there are singing parties—the special s.f. songs. The con suite (of the fan group that sponsors the con) usually has an open house, but mainly for its group members, certain other fans, and, of course, the pros.

Pros are welcome at any party given by a fan. The pro parties, however, are strictly by invitation only and are closed unless you are brought in by a friend of that pro. Pro invitations are not only to other pros, but to fans as well—most of the time. There are certain pros who have very restricted parties.

The parties go on until the wee hours of the morning.

Despite all the drinking, s.f. people rarely get all that drunk—it is impossible to have a conversation when you can't talk. Con attendees rarely cause trouble for a hotel, and therefore the cons are high on the hotel list of convention ratings.

On Sunday the programs start again, in the late morning, and there is also an art auction. The con is officially over at around

4:00 p.m. However, most hotels have very early checkout times, and this sometimes causes some inconvenience when you're trying to check out on time and still see the rest of the con. Most people go home after the official closing, but there are hardy ones who stay and party another night.

Conventions are a business. They make money for their sponsors. There have been controversies as to whether the writers should be paid for appearing on the programs. Fans feel that the publicity that the writers get, the promotion for their work, is payment enough. The writers feel that it is their time that is valuable. In the early days conventions sometimes didn't make their expenses, and writers helped pass the hat to raise enough money. Today, very few cons, if any, fail to make a profit. There is money from the attendance and huckster fees, and the sponsors also get a percentage of the room rates the hotel charges.

The conventions with the most attendees (10,000) are the "Star Trek" cons, but not all of those attendees are part of the s.f. community. The largest s.f. con, the Worldcon, has had as many as five thousand attendees. Major conventions can also have several thousand attendees. If you have never attended a s.f. convention, go to a smaller con first. Don't start with the Worldcon. You will have a chance to experience the atmosphere of a con and get to know some regulars, both fans and pros. Then, when you go to a large con, there will be familiar faces, and you will also be known. This will help you meet the other people and become a community member.

How do you get to meet and know people at a con? Just go over to someone and introduce yourself, start a conversation. Everyone is friendly.

8

The S.F. Writers' Organizations

The Science Fiction Writers of America, Inc., was founded in 1965 and recently became incorporated. It has a membership of approximately 500, of which 90 percent are writers. The organization accepts members from all countries, but its membership is primarily in the English-language countries. It has no office address or telephone number. The only way to contact SFWA is through its executive secretary.

Every fan within the s.f. community who is an aspiring writer wants to be a member of SFWA.

Qualifying for the yearly membership as a writer depends on the type and amount of fiction published. There are three classes of membership: active, affiliate, and institutional.

Institutional does not apply to the writers of fiction, just those organizations that have an interest in s.f. (such as a university) or people associated with such an institution.

Affiliate members are of two categories: those with an "abiding professional concern" with s.f. (agents, editors, etc.); and beginning writers, those who have sold at least one piece of science fiction.

Active membership requirements are based on the "sale and publication" on a professional basis of at least three shorter s.f. (or fantasy) works or one longer work. A longer work can be a novel, TV script, screenplay, or longer radio script. The works can have been published any time prior to application. Also eligible for active membership are professional s.f. artists, although they have their own professional organization. Once you have qualified for active status, you can remain an active member just as long as you pay your yearly dues.

The annual dues are $40 for active members, $25 for affiliate members (plus a one-time "processing" fee of $7.50), and $40 for institutional members.

Only active members can receive the *SFWA Forum*, nominate, vote, run for a SFWA office, or recommend and vote for Nebula Awards. All members can attend SFWA meetings.

The SFWA elected officers are president, vice-president, secretary, and treasurer. They serve one-year terms. There are four elected regional directors, who serve staggered three-year terms. The eastern, south/central, and western regions refer to the United States, though the sectors also include Canada and Mexico; the overseas region is primarily Europe and also Japan (Australia and New Zealand are not within this area and are already represented). The executive secretary is appointed (or volunteers) and is the contact for SFWA. The current executive secretary is:

> Peter Pautz
> 68 Countryside Apts.
> Hackettstown, NJ 07840
> Phone: (201) 852-8531

SFWA has various committees and trustees, and offers writers advice and many services regarding the profession of writing and s.f. in particular. The organization has several publications, including the *Nebula Awards Anthology* (issued annually); and the *SFWA Handbook,* which is a guide for s.f. writers and includes model contracts and the SFWA bylaws. The handbook is available to nonmembers for $5.

There is also a *SFWA Directory,* which lists all SFWA members' names, addresses, and agents (available to nonmembers for $25); *The Bulletin,* a slick publication in a magazine format and the official organ of SFWA, published quarterly (nonmembers may subscribe at $10 for four issues); and the *SFWA Forum,* a publication that allows members to air their opinions and grievances in an informal manner—which is why it goes only to active members.

Although the regional directors may hold meetings in their areas, SFWA holds only two regular business meetings each year—in April, at the Nebula Awards weekend, and on the Labor Day weekend at the Worldcon. If enough members are expected to be at a particular major s.f. convention, a meeting is scheduled at that con. Otherwise, the only contact most members have with each other is through either the *Bulletin* or the *SFWA Forum.*

If you can qualify for membership, write to the SFWA membership chairman, requesting a membership application, and enclose an SASE:

> Somtow Sucharitkul
> 16 Ancell Street
> Alexandria, VA 22305

SFWA publishes a pamphlet describing the organization. It is currently out of print but may be updated and reissued. Should it again become available, it would be obtainable from the executive secretary with an SASE.

The best way to get ahead in the organization is to volunteer to do something once you are a member. Although some of the tasks can be done only by active members, even an affiliate member can be of enormous help to the organization. It will also put you in contact with those who can advance your writing career. You may hear market news first, of which you could take advantage.

As in any organization, there are politics and cliques, and

though the organization itself presents a solid front to the outside—including the fans—there are internal disagreements concerning organizational matters as well as personality clashes. A few members are far more outspoken than others. If you can qualify as an active member, this will become apparent with your very first issue of the *SFWA Forum*.

There are s.f. writers' organizations in other countries, which are limited to its citizens. In England there is the British Science Fiction Association, Ltd. (BSFA), which had its beginnings in 1958. It has its own publications and, like SFWA, gives awards, but, until recently, only to their own members. Some of the BSFA members are also SFWA members, but this is basically a United Kingdom organization.

There has been an attempt to organize a true international s.f. professional group, the World SF, but it is still in its formational stages. This may eventually become a viable professional organization.

9

The Awards

Many awards are given to professionals, by both the professional organizations and the fans. To a writer, winning an award means money—his fiction will generate more sales if a book (or magazine) can advertise the fact that the writer has won a prestigious award.

Winning an award does not always mean that the fiction was better than its contenders. Politics have a lot to do with an award. If you have done a lot for an organization, you may be rewarded by a nomination—and sometimes awards can be won for just such a reason. If you are popular with the fans—by appearing in a lot of programs on panels or by being somewhat theatrical in your speeches (doing your "act")—you could also win an award over an equally qualified contender. And, if you constantly tell the s.f. community what a great writer you are, and how wonderfully superior your fiction is, they just might eventually believe you and give you awards.

The most coveted and best known awards are the Nebula and Hugo.

The Nebula

Presented by SFWA at its annual Nebula Awards Banquet, the award is a block of lucite in which are embedded a spiral nebula (the word should really be *galaxy*) made of metallic glitter and a specimen of quartz crystal. It is handmade, and no two are exactly alike.

They are spectacularly beautiful. They are also rather delicate and have, on occasion, cracked while in transit.

The fiction is nominated by SFWA members, and the nominees are selected through a three-step process including a Nebula Jury, which may add its own recommendations to the final ballot. The works are then voted on by only the active members. Awards are given in the categories of novel, novella, novelette, and short story. There are also awards for Best Dramatic Presentation, but this is not given every year. SFWA also gives a Grand Master Award, but this is for a lifetime of writing achievement and is not a Nebula. While the Nebula can theoretically be given to any writer, it usually goes to a SFWA member.

The Hugo

This is the annual Worldcon Award, presented by the *attendees;* that is, the registered members. This means that fans and pros alike, and some people who never read s.f., vote for the awards. The Hugo Award is a stylized rocket ship resting on its tail fins and mounted on a wooden block. It is named after Hugo Gernsback, the "father" of modern science fiction, and has been presented since 1953. Because these awards are given primarily by fans, this is considered a fan award. The categories are: novel, novella, novelette, and short story. There is also an award for best dramatic presentation, professional artist, professional editor, nonfiction book about some aspect of s.f., fanzine, fan writer, and fan artist. Once again, theoretically any s.f. writer can win, but the awards are usually give to SFWA writers.

The John W. Campbell Award

Presented annually at the Worldcon through the same voting method as the Hugos, this award is for the best s.f. writer of the year. Named after the great editor, this award has been presented since 1972, sponsored by the publishers of *Analog*.

The Gandalf Award

This award for fantasy fiction is also presented at the Worldcon.

The World Fantasy Award

Presented annually at the World Fantasy Convention, it is voted on by registered members only. The award is not called by any name, as are the Hugo and Nebula. It is a pewter bust of H.P. Lovecraft, which was designed by the artist Gahan Wilson. Only living persons are eligible for the award. The categories are: novel, short fiction, anthology or collection, special awards (one pro, one nonpro), and life achievement. Awards are given to writers, editors, and artists. "Special" awards may be given for a nonfiction work, or to a professional or nonprofessional writer or publisher.

The John W. Campbell Memorial Award

Presented annually for the best s.f. novel of the year published in the English language, this award is often confused with the other Campbell Award. Although it originated in the United States in 1973, it is administered now in the United Kingdom. The selections are made by a committee consisting of both s.f.

writers and academe, and it is not voted on; merely chosen.

The Jupiter

Presented annually, this award is administered by SFRA and is an illuminated scroll. Categories are novel, novella, novelette, and short story. This is an award given by the academe.

The Pilgrim

Presented annually, this is another award by the academe, sponsored by SFRA since 1970 and given at its annual conference. The award is made by selection, and those who receive it become honorary SFRA members. The Pilgrim is given for s.f. scholarship and criticism.

The Balrog

Presented annually at the Fool-Con held over Easter weekend at the Johnson County Community College, Overland Park, Kansas, the award is a small statue by Jeff Easley. Anyone can make a nomination, and anyone can vote. The awards are only for a specific type of fantasy—sword & sorcery (which they also call *heroic fantasy*), horror (called *dark fantasy*), "sword and planet à la Burroughs," and fantasy as in the fantasy of Tolkien. Within this range of fantasy categories, the awards categories are novel, short fiction, collection/anthology, best poet, best artist, and outstanding pro achievement. There is also a Special Award made by a panel of judges. Additionally, there are two film Balrogs, one for fantasy and one for science fiction, which are Balrog Hall of Fame awards. The film awards are plaques.

The Rhysling

Presented annually by SFPA, the award is named after the blind poet created by Heinlein. The categories are long poem and short poem. Poetry is not, unfortunately, a category in the other s.f. and fantasy awards, the sole exception being the Balrog, which puts the Rhysling on a par with the Hugo and Nebula.

The Grey Mauser

Presented annually at the Fantasy Faire, this award for outstanding contributions to adult fantasy is named after the creation of Fritz Leiber. The award is a replica of a Mauser pistol.

The Ditmar

Presented at the annual Australian National S.F. Convention, the award, equal to the Hugo, is basically limited to Australian recipients. The awards are also voted on in the same manner as the Hugos. The award category outside the national ones is for best international fiction. The William Atheling Award is also given.

The BSFA Award

Presented annually at the BSFA Easter Convention, they have been given since 1981 for works first published and/or presented in the United Kingdom. They were formerly a national award only. BSFA is a writers' organization, and this is a pro award. The categories are novel, short fiction, media presentation, and artist.

The British Fantasy Awards

Presented at the annual British Fantasycon, these awards can be won by anyone but are mainly national. Categories are novel, short fiction, small press publication, film, artist, and comic (book or strip).

The August Derleth Award

Presented by the British Fantasy Society, the award is international.

There are other national awards and special memorial awards given by professional organizations (such as the Japanese Science Fiction Writers group) and fan groups and also s.f. film awards.

10

Publications

There are several hundred fan publications, known as *fanzines*—a combination of *fan* and maga*zine*. Certain of these fanzines will pay for stories or articles by writers at a low rate of ½¢ to 3¢ and more a word. Publication in a fanzine will *not* give you professional status to qualify for SFWA. But it is a method of getting your work in print and being paid for it.

A fanzine can be a photocopied typed sheet, a few mimeographed stapled sheets, or a slick-paper, professional-looking magazine. Fanzines contain news of interest to fandom—opinions, critiques, and book reviews.

But there is another type of publication that transcends the fanzines and can only be called *newszines*. And this is where the value of the s.f. community becomes so apparent to a writer. This is what is so very vital to any writer—aspiring, beginning, or long established. Newszines are unique to science fiction. They do not, and cannot, exist in any other field.

There are two newszines: *Locus* and *Science Fiction Chronicle* (known as *SF Chronicle*). Published monthly, they are similar in some ways, yet different in others.

Locus is more fan oriented, and *SF Chronicle* leans more toward the professional side of s.f. *SF Chronicle* is typeset and slicker in appearance. Its editor and publisher, Andrew (Andy) Porter has worked on professional magazines for many years and was an assistant editor of *F&SF*. Charles (Charlie) N. Brown, the editor and publisher of *Locus,* started his publication as a fanzine and it evolved into a newszine. Charlie Brown is considered a professional as well, as he writes articles in pro publications and is a small press publisher. Andy Porter also publishes a slick semipro fanzine, *Starship: The Magazine About SF,* which is entirely nonfiction. A small press publisher, he owns the Algol Press.

Both newszines are international in scope and distribution. They contain photographs, news of the community (both fan and pro), obituaries, and publishing news; marketing information and news; ads of the pro book publishers, both large and small, ads of conventions, semipro fanzines, and s.f. organizations; classified ads; a listing of the monthly releases by large and small publishing houses (pro and semipro) and specialized publications (including book and magazine releases); articles; a listing of conventions with con information; reports on the events in the s.f. community, both fan and pro; award winner listings; reports on the major conventions, including non–s.f. conventions such as the American Booksellers Association; book reviews; letters; and articles relating to the genre, the professional side of the genre, and the business side of writing. Despite this similarity, it is the manner of presentation and the exact contents within each newszine that makes them different.

Locus lists the monthly releases (books) alphabetically by the name of the writer, which is important to a reader. *SF Chronicle* lists these releases, including the contents of the pro magazines, alphabetically, but by the name of the publisher (or magazine), which is useful to a writer, especially an aspiring writer, as it gives some indication as to which publishing houses issue the greatest number of titles and which are the most active in the field. *Locus* lists an enormous amount of conventions (with related information), while *SF Chronicle* lists only the major cons. *Locus* has a monthly bestseller list (just like *The New York Times Book Review*), which is compiled from information obtained from the many s.f. bookshops in North America. It also publishes the results of an all-encompassing yearly s.f. poll of its subscribers, as well as a yearly book summary listing by publishers. Each January, May, and September, *SF Chronicle* has an in-depth market report of all types of publishers—book, anthology, fanzines that pay, genre magazines, game magazines, and general-topic magazines. Book publishers are listed separately under hardcover and paperback. *Locus* runs more articles basically oriented to writers than *SF Chronicle;* on the other hand, Andy Porter's *Starship* also publishes these types of articles as well as other nonfiction pieces. *SF Chronicle* has a regular film column.

Both newszines give you *instantaneous* news occurring within the community—and the publishing news is of the utmost importance to any writer. It is only in these newszines that you can get marketing information on anthologies, both continuing and one-time, both reprint and original. New publishing houses come into existence, new publishers join the field, new magazines come into existence, and a writer can learn of this immediately and in detail. Editors constantly change their jobs—sometimes this is referred to as "musical editors." No other marketing publications can possibly keep up with all this specialized news in so rapid a reporting time. Even this book cannot do more than list the continuing series original anthologies, as the one-time originals are too limited in a time span to list fairly.

Since the SFWA *Bulletin* is quarterly and the *SFWA Forum* is only for active members (and is published erratically), the two newszines scoop the SFWA publications on the marketing news, making these two newszines virtually the earliest sources of current marketing information and news available to SFWA writers and the only sources available to a writer who is not a member of SFWA.

Which newszine is best for you? Only you can decide—and it might be both. It is suggested that you request a sample issue of *SF Chronicle* and *Locus* (which should cost about $1.50 and $2.00, respectively); inquire about cost with an SASE. Ask for the most recent issue of each publication. You might also wish to obtain the latest market report issue (January, May, or September) of *SF Chronicle*. Then you will be able to ascertain which newszine you prefer and if you want a subscription. It is also suggested that, if you do subscribe to one, you subscribe to the other, too.

Their addresses are as follows:

S.F. Chronicle
P.O. Box 4175
New York, NY 10163

Locus Publications
P.O. Box 3938
San Francisco, CA 94119

PART III: THE PROFESSIONAL MANUSCRIPT—PREPARATION AND SUBMISSIONS

11

What Do Editors Look For?

Although all publishers desire to publish work that brings critical acclaim to their authors and themselves, the hard fact of the matter is that they are in business to make money. Without financial success, a publisher would not be able to continue in the field. Therefore, the publisher hires capable editors who not only know their market but use artistic judgment tempered with practical, down-to-earth thinking in order to assure that the pages coming off the press invite sales.

Editors look for well-written stories that are tightly plotted, whose characters are more than cardboard or two-dimensional.

Even as you and I, editors dream, too. They constantly hope to discover a new writer who will consistently send them quality manuscripts that will result in huge sales and win awards—a writer who might become a literary superstar and remain loyal to them.

Magazine editors, who have an established subscription market and established and "name" writers to carry each issue, are in a better position than book companies to take a chance on an unknown writer and first-time publication. Therefore, if you can produce fiction that fits within the framework of a particular magazine—or more than one—an editor might take a chance on you. Anthologies, too, have a sufficient number of well-known writers to allow their editors to accept new, unknown writers' work, and there are anthologies containing stories entirely by new writers that even include first stories.

Many of the s.f. magazines are proud to publish a story by a new writer—and preface it with an introduction announcing that the author's work is seeing print for the first time. Then, when that magazine publishes subsequent stories by the same author, they will note that fact.

The situation with a book publisher, however, is different. It is risky to publish a novel by a new writer whose efforts have never been in print in the genre before or, for that matter, in any other literary category. However, if an editor really believes in you and in your ability, as well as in your book, he will take that chance, even during poor market conditions. Sometimes an editor will go to bat for you with higher-ups to get a book published.

Should an editor offer to work with you, help you, or suggest rewriting until a novel that is close but not quite "there" is potentially acceptable for publication, do not refuse the offer. It might develop into your first sale.

Some editors or publishers might state in articles, at conventions, writers' conferences, or elsewhere what their wants are, yet later ignore these restrictions. This is because a story or novel manuscript that showed up was so good that it could not be ignored. Thus, a magazine that is known for and usually publishes hard s.f. may receive a story bordering on fantasy by a first-time writer—and buy it!

This, however, is the exception. It is alway best to stick to announced requirements.

Such a contradictory acceptance for a book publisher might also be a reaction to a change in the market. Or it could be the result of replacement in editorship by someone who has a different set of requirements.

In s.f., editors—especially those in book publishing—change jobs fairly often but usually stay within the genre. Also, first readers and editorial assistants advance and become editors. New magazines come into existence, and a well-known writer may become one of the editors.

Because a particular editor's taste or viewpoint may be the basis for acceptance or rejection of a manuscript, it is a good idea to keep track of the markets and which editor is where. An editor who sent you that encouraging rejection slip with the comment: "Well written, but unfortunately not for us" may now be working for the publisher for whom your piece is just right—or might be more responsive to your new submission.

A story may be "ahead of its time." Even in science fiction this can be true. A story may wait many years for publication because, for example, its subject matter is taboo when it is written. Another reason might be that a scientific or technological development makes a highly advanced and imaginative story more plausible to the reader.

A good story will usually, in time, find a publisher—if it is submitted often enough.

A rejection slip is not necessarily final.

12
Appearance, Format, and Length

Appealing Physical Appearance

If you intend to submit short stories or novels to editors and wish to have them seriously considered, it is necessary that their appearance be professional.

A good 16- to 20-pound bond paper is suitable. Typing errors can be corrected best through the use of type-over paper or correction fluid, obtainable at a stationery store. Careful erasing, without producing holes, is satisfactory, however.

A manuscript should always be typed, never handwritten. An electric typewriter is not a necessity. Any typewriter will do, as long as it produces neat, legible, easy-to-read pages.

Should it be necessary for you to buy a typewriter, you will find that used ones can be obtained at extremely reasonable prices. They can be found not only at typewriter repair stores that specialize in selling, too, but at flea markets and garage sales as well.

There are two sizes of type—pica (large) and elite (small).

Although the larger is easier on the editors' eyes, both are acceptable.

Before typing a final manuscript, be certain that your keys are clean. Dust and erasure particles mixed with ribbon ink accumulates as guck inside some letters, such as the *es* and *os*. So you should clean your keys regularly. This can be done simply and inexpensively with household rubbing alcohol and a toothbrush or piece of cloth. The insides of the letters can be cleaned with a toothpick, pin, or cotton swab. You can also buy a special gum-rubber kit made specifically for this purpose. Be careful that the ink doesn't get onto your clothes.

An editor's job includes the reading of many submissions and those manuscripts whose letters are dark have an advantage over those that are lightly typed. Be certain to use a ribbon that is not worn out.

If you are unable to do a good typing job on your manuscript, there are a number of alternatives you can take. Friends, neighbors, or relatives might be able to help you. If not, a notice put up on the bulletin board of your local supermarket, high school, or college might bring you a typist who will work at a reasonable rate. If none of these means is available, there are typing services that advertise in the writers' trade magazines. Professional work is done by these people, and corrections (not editing) of your rough draft are usually included. In addition, some offer a choice of type style. And you will be provided with a carbon copy. However, your wait for the finished product will include the two-way postal delivery. And you might find the cost prohibitive. A positive note is that some of these services will accept cassette recordings.

Recognized Format

A professional manuscript (known to writers and editors as an *ms* or *MS*—or, in the plural, *mss* or *MSS*) should have a border on all four sides of about one or one-and-a-half inches. A cramped page can be discouraging to an editor.

Double-space the lines. This makes your submission easy to read for both the reader and—if you sell it—the typesetter.

In the upper left-hand corner of the first page, type your name and address. Addition of your phone number is optional. Should the manuscript sell, the name (or names) noted here will be on the letter of acceptance, contract, or check.

Type an approximation of the number of words in your ms at the upper right-hand corner. The figure is arrived at by rounding off your actual count. If, for example, your story is 5,274 words, type: Approx. 5,300 words.

If you are a member of The Science Fiction Writers of America, add "Member SFWA" under your name or the word count. Place that statement on the envelope, too. This will put the reading of your work before that of the unsolicited manuscripts, known as the *slush pile,* and bring it to the immediate attention of the editor.

If you are represented by an agent, you can also add that information to the manuscript. Alternatively, you can state that fact in a covering letter. Or you can wait until the sale before informing the editor.

Should you wish to put a copyright notice on your manuscript, you will find instructions on this procedure in the section on copyright in this guide.

Your title goes about halfway down the page. Beneath that, double-spaced, put "by" (centered) and, after another double space, the name you wish to appear as the author—yours or a pen name. Then, after about four lines, begin the story.

The first page is half blank for the purpose of editorial comments regarding type size and style, headings and other related "copy" (text) or instruction to the typesetter.

The following pages of the ms may be numbered at the center or right top; your last name should appear at the left.

The end of the story is simply indicated with the term *The End.* Or, you may prefer to use the traditional symbols: *30* or *XXX.*

In a novel manuscript, the text begins on the second page—

following the title page, which would be set up as described above.

When indicating words to be italicized, underline the word, words, or lines.

Should You Use a Pen Name?

Depending on your own personal situation and outlook, you may or may not want to use your own name on that first ms page.

A number of science fiction writers who are established in the field resent being in the s.f. ghetto. They feel that their work is looked down on because it is science fiction and therefore not as "worthy" a literature as mainstream. In addition, it is their opinion that being labeled as s.f. writers closes opportunities in many other areas of writing to them.

Some writers are concerned that their readers, who, as trusting followers, have become accustomed to buying books and magazines promoting that particular author's name for genre works, would be displeased to discover that they had purchased writing of theirs not in the category of fiction they expected.

Many writers of s.f. are actually professional scientists—with Ph.D. after their names—and may publish scientific papers. Some may not want their serious or even scholarly work to be confused with their fiction—or perhaps have their nonfiction made light of just because they happen to write s.f.

Also, there are writers in other professions—such as law, as attorneys or judges—who would not want a general public knowledge of their fiction writing to have an adverse effect on their professional lives.

And then there are many writers having jobs whose employers might assume they were writing fiction—or even thinking about writing it—on company time. There are some employers who are strongly opposed to any form of mental activity that is not job-related, though they may not feel the same way about sports activities. In fact, employers exist who feel that their employees should devote all of their mental energies to business, even when not at the office. On the other hand, an employer may take advantage of the fact that you can write by having you do company speeches or reports on your own thinking time!

Therefore, since you may not want an employer to learn that you have abilities that you're using for your own benefit, you may wish to write under a pen name.

Some writers, for one reason or another, prefer privacy in their personal lives; they like to keep their personal and literary professional lives separate.

What Should Be the Length of a Manuscript?

Science fiction stories usually run from about 500 to 5,000 words, though some are much shorter than 500 and others can run to 7,500.

The Science Fiction Writers of America, Inc., for the purpose of categorizing its annual Nebula Award nominees, stipulates a short story as having a word length of up to 7,500; a novelette, 7,500 to 17,500; a novella, 17,500 to 40,000; and a novel, 40,000 and more.

Magazine editors often pay more per word for short-short stories—considered to be in the range of 1,000 words—than for regular length fiction.

It is important that you be thoroughly familiar with the story wordage used by the magazine to which you wish to submit your manuscript, especially the s.f. magazines. These word lengths may vary considerably within an issue, but if you examine the past six or so, you will probably find a certain consistency.

When you have a representative number of issues of the magazine to which you wish to submit a story, you can count the number of words in each of its stories and calculate the average. This can easily be accomplished.

First, count the words in several lines of a story and take an average. Figure out the number of lines that total closest to 100 words. Then, with your thumb and forefinger, a ruler, or a marked piece of paper, measure that 100-word distance down the column you have just computed. Move this measurement through the pages of the story, counting off the wordage in hundreds.

In the final analysis, however, you should not be overly concerned about the number of words in your manuscript; this can restrict creativity. A story should dictate its own length. You don't want to pad the story with excess and uninteresting writing; neither do you want to delete important parts. An honestly written story should have a better chance of selling than one whose prose has been manipulated to fit an arbitrary length. If it does grab the editor but is not the proper length for that publication, be assured that you will be asked to make adjustments.

To estimate the number of words in a novel, as with the short stories, average the number of words on a line. By flipping through the book you can get a general idea of the length of the average line with respect to dialogue and quotations. Then, reckon the number of pages that are partially blank at the beginnings and ends of chapters. Finally, taking into consideration all of these factors, figure out the average wordage per page, multiply that by the last numbered page of text, and subtract your appraisal of total blank pages.

Book publishers, as noted in the market listings in this guide, usually have preferred word-length ranges, dictated by production costs and book prices. Occasionally, they may publish a novel of a length that is inconsistent with their usual practice—when these have been written by established "name" writers in the genre.

Counting YOUR Words

For a short story of just a few pages, count each word—which can be done quickly—and round the total off at the nearest hundred. However, should the piece run longer, perhaps five pages or more, wordage can be more easily estimated.

Estimate wordage on longer mss by selecting a number of

typical full lines at random—then average them. Should your count be ten to fourteen words per line, make it twelve. Next, go through your ms and count the number of full lines, adding partial lines together to count as margin-to-margin ones. Then, multiply these figures.

For a longer work, such as a novelette or novel, you might find it more expedient to count the words on a typical page having an average look of dialogue and narrative and then multiply that total by the number of pages in your manuscript.

Using this average-words-per-page number—which, depending on whether your typewriter has elite or pica type, may run from 250 to 350 words—you will probably be able to estimate all of your manuscripts with ease.

13

Handling the Manuscript Pages

Preventing Loss of Your Labors

Before sending out any manuscript, be certain that you have a duplicate of it—either carbon copies or photocopies of its pages.

Although it isn't likely that your original manuscript will be lost in the mail, it could happen. Other causes of its disappearance could be:

- An editor could misplace it and, despite your letters or phone queries, not be able to locate it.
- A publisher might hold it and never return it, not replying to your desperate queries.

If you've sent your only copy and it is not returned, it will be gone forever. You will never be able to write it exactly the same way again.

Never send out your work without retaining a copy.

Photocopied Submissions/Multiple (Simultaneous) Submissions

A manuscript that has done a lot of traveling through the

mail and has been handled by many editors eventually begins to show signs of wear. It is not to your advantage to keep sending it out.

If you've been submitting a photocopy, all you need do is make another set from the pages of your mint-condition original, filed safely at home.

However, many magazine editors—especially those in the s.f. genre—do not read photocopied submissions. Book editors will sometimes consider a photocopy, but only after the writer has queried regarding such a submission.

Although a few magazine editors may find photocopied manuscripts acceptable, you must, as a rule, submit original manuscripts to them. It is best to query about photocopies.

Most editors, especially those of s.f. magazines and anthologies, understandably, do not care to invest their time in considering multiple submissions—that is, manuscripts that are sent simultaneously to more than one publisher—only to have one suddenly withdrawn by the author because it has been accepted by someone else. In the case of an editor who is employed full-time by a publisher, the publisher would be investing editorial costs that would involve additional personnel and overhead costs.

Only a few book publishers accept multiple submissions. Most prefer exclusive consideration of a manuscript. And keep in mind that a photocopy implies a simultaneous submission unless your purpose is explained in a covering letter.

Nevertheless, there is the writer's side of the situation. And, fortunately, there is a trend toward a more liberal attitude on the part of publishers regarding multiple submissions. This is much to the advantage of the unagented author who, with waiting periods each of which could last for months, would barely be allowed a reasonable number of tries—in a year's time or even longer—to locate an interested publisher.

Should you consider making a photocopied and/or simultaneous submission, check the market reports regarding acceptability with the publisher. If this information is not available, query.

Then, when submitting a manuscript under either or both conditions—photocopied or multiple—include a covering letter stating that fact.

Attaching Manuscript Pages

The typed pages of your short story or novel should never be stapled together. Neither should they have holes punched into them for fastening with rings or other devices.

The pages should be loose so that the editor—and typesetter—can easily deal with one at a time.

A manuscript that is not too thick, as one of a short story, can be fastened together with a paper clip. If you wish to prevent indentation that might suggest a round of rejections to subsequent editors, a card or piece of paper folded several times can be placed under the clip. (Your indentation-protector, of course, may not be used on the return trip.)

Retyping may eventually be necessary—at least of the first page—if a number of paper clip indentations are made.

A novel is sent loose, in a box. See "Submitting the Manuscript," Chapter 15.

14

Querying the Editor

The Short Story

Unless you are inquiring about submitting a photocopy instead of the original, or about a simultaneous submission, it is unnecessary to query a magazine editor. However, the situation is often different with anthologies (short stories by different authors, as opposed to collections that are the work of one author), which are often based on single themes.

An anthologist may set a specific date beyond which manuscripts will no longer be considered, especially for an anthology that is not one of a continuing series. Continuing series anthologists may sometimes accept a manuscript beyond the closing date for possible inclusion in the next book.

There are different types of reprint anthologies. The best-of-the-year kinds are not, of course, generally open to submissions. Neither are those of noted authors or editors who have usually preselected the works before approaching a publisher or who, after contracting for publication, look to established authors for material.

However, often there are anthology announcements for reprints and even originals for the work of new authors. In such cases multiple submissions might be considered when a story has already been published elsewhere.

When inquiring in such cases as those noted above, provide the editor with any background information that will work to your advantage. This might pertain to work that you have published or that is being seriously considered—and not necessarily just in science fiction. Also, if you are involved in activities with SFWA or science fiction conventions, note that fact. Then give a brief description of what you wish to submit, noting its theme and length and perhaps including a plot description of a few sentences. Enclosure of an SASE would be an appreciated courtesy.

The Novel

As noted in Chapter 20 on book markets, many publishers are now requesting query letters before the submission of a manuscript, whether it is for the complete work or for three chapters and an outline. The requirement is especially applicable to unpublished writers and those without agents. These letters should include a brief description of your background—education (including workshops or conferences), publishing, writing, and related experience, and other facts regarding your proposed submission. In addition, a description of the theme of your book should be included (not to be confused with the plot, or story line), plus a somewhat detailed description of the plot. You should also ask about photocopies and exclusive or multiple submissions if you are considering going these routes.

Keep your letter as brief as possible, yet make it long enough to interest the editor.

No matter how many queries you make simultaneously, each letter should provide a personal touch by being an original. The theme and plot description may be carbon copies or photocopies.

If you are just starting out as a writer, it would be to your benefit to complete your entire book before querying. Should your receive a response of interest in your work, it would be much to your advantage to submit the polished piece immediately while there is interest and obviously a publishing schedule into which your work might fit. Being able to show only a good idea or a rough first draft of a few chapters might work against you.

If your query informed the editor that you have three chapters and an outline, they should already be professionally done and ready to submit. An editor will judge you as a writer on the basis of your initial submission, even if it is incomplete. The criteria will be how well it is written and how neatly it is presented.

Don't bank on being able, without experience, to come up quickly with quality work—even if it may be a partial manuscript. There are, of course, established professional writers who, when interest is expressed by an editor, can adjust their schedules and turn out a sparkling piece in a short time.

If the same doors of opportunity open to you and you need an inordinate amount of time (around a job) to come through, the picture at the publishing house could easlily change. Another book might be taken in place of yours, a new direction in publishing strategy might evolve, or you might find that when your manuscript is finally completed and submitted it will be read and considered by another editor.

A Time Limit for a Query Response?

Most editors try to answer writers as soon as possible, but they should be allowed at least a month. Editors must contend with a great many queries at their offices—and sometimes homes.

You should receive a reply to your letter within a period of a few days to a month. Should you not hear within a reasonable time, inquire again, mentioning the date and content of your original query. You might enclose an SASE as a courtesy.

What to Expect on a Query Reply

Naturally, if you asked about whether photocopies and/or

multiple submissions are acceptable, you'll be advised of the editor's policies on that; any of your other questions should also be answered.

Should your query be about the submission of a novel, if you don't receive a definite rejection, you will be asked to send your work. The request might be for a sample chapter, a few chapters and an outline, or your entire manuscript.

Subsequent submission of a partial manuscript that interests the editor should get you an invitation to send the entire book.

Should You Include a Covering Letter?

A covering letter to a magazine editor or anthologist is unnecessary if all you have to say is, "I'm submitting this manuscript."

If you wish to have a copyright notice in your name published with your story, should it be accepted, this should be requested in a letter. For details involving this situation, see Chapter 19 on "Legal and Financial Matters."

It is a good idea to file carbon copies of your letters in their respective manuscript folders. This will provide a quick reference to the name of any magazine or anthology editor to whom you've submitted your work, addresses, dates, titles, and other related information. Or you might wish to handle this data more easily with a record book.

Should you be encouraged by an editor with a printed rejection slip having on it a personal comment of the well-written-but-not-for-us/please-try-us-again type, be sure to refer to it on your next submission to that editor.

If you have any publishing credits—even one—let the editor know in a covering letter. Once you've sold, always send a letter mentioning that fact, including the name of the magazine or book publisher, the title of the work, and the publication date. This will let the editor—or especially the first reader—know that you're a professional writer (a person who has had writing published and paid for). In time—with persistence on your part—one sale should lead to another, and you will be able to list more and more credits, to which you should add other literary-related accomplishments and activities: articles and other nonfiction, fillers, poetry, etc. Make photocopies of a credit sheet, for inclusion with your manuscripts. And update it at every opportunity. You can enclose a brief covering letter and refer to this list.

Should you address a manuscript to any specific person at a magazine?

Science fiction genre magazine mastheads will list an editor and sometimes also a managing editor. In other magazines a fiction editor may be listed or just the editor. If there is a fiction editor, send your manuscript to that person; otherwise, submit it to the editor.

Whether you include a covering letter or not, it will most likely be more to your advantage to write to a person rather than address it impersonally to "The Editor."

It is a good idea to include a covering letter with your novel manuscript, especially should it be submitted in response to an invitation resulting from a query. In the latter situation, it will inform the person who opens the package that your work was solicited and should receive priority treatment.

Should an editor request only three chapters and an outline, despite the fact that your manuscript may be completed, do not send more. The reason that this small sample of your writing abilities was requested is that the editor's time is limited. And the outline should be done separately, not as a part of the covering letter.

15

Submitting the Manuscript

Sending Your Manuscript Off

A short manuscript of just two or three pages can be folded into thirds and mailed in a business (#10) envelope. Included with it should be an SASE (self-addressed stamped envelope).

A longer manuscript is better submitted in a 9" × 12" manila envelope, which will hold standard 8½" × 11" typing paper without risk of cramping and creasing it. You may prefer this size for the shorter manuscripts, too, if you would rather not fold them.

Additional protection can be provided by including a piece of 8½" × 11" cardboard (from the back of a pad or cut from a corrugated cardboard box), even though it will add extra weight (about 1 ounce) and therefore require additional postage. This helps prevent creasing and mangling in its journey, which may (hopefully not) be two-way.

A poorly protected manuscript that is returned sometimes requires retyping, if you don't want the next editor to feel that you're submitting rejected material. A fresh manuscript gives a fresh impression.

An SASE should always be enclosed with a submission—not only as a courtesy. Some editors will not return manuscripts without them.

You may connect with an editor who buys your work and tells you not to enclose an SASE.

You may be contacted by an editor who for some reason— perhaps having seen a story of yours in print—requests a manuscript from you. If so, this would be considered a solicited manuscript, not requiring you to enclose an SASE.

Otherwise, most submissions are unsolicited manuscripts and should be accompanied by a return envelope. If even the largest-circulation magazines or major publishers had to pay return postage for their rejections, because of the number of submissions received, the cost would be felt.

Naturally, if an editor requests your manuscript in reply to a query, you should enclose return postage.

To mail a novel manuscript, you can use a cardboard box, which a ream (500 sheets) of bond came in. It can be taped and enclosed in brown wrapping paper. In place of a box, a corrugated cardboard box can be cut into pieces to fit the six sides of the typescript.

At your local stationery store you can obtain large, padded mailing envelopes. These can be used easily. You just slide the manuscript in and staple the side.

Be certain that, when you weigh your manuscript to send it out, you do it twice—once with one envelope and again with two. The weight with two envelopes will determine the cost of sending it out—with the return envelope folded inside and possibly used to prevent manuscript indentation by the paper clip.

The return trip would be calculated for one envelope. A 9 " × 12" envelope weighs about one ounce; therefore, the difference between postage on both envelopes is usually about the cost of a one-ounce letter.

Of course, you can weigh your submissions for free at the post office. However, it is more convenient to obtain an inexpensive scale that measures up to one or two pounds, which will save you trips to the post office.

For novels, there are scales that can accommodate four or five pounds. Nevertheless, a small scale can be used to weigh the typescript in sections, which can then be totaled.

Although you can send your manuscript by a cheaper rate than first class, the slight difference for a few ounces may not be worth the savings. The time and cost of retyping the manuscript after a brutal trip might not be worth it.

United Parcel Service (UPS) has reasonable rates—especially if there is an office near you and pickup is not required.

If you wish to insure your manuscript, only the value of the physical material can be covered. In other words, you may insure it for the cost of the paper and typing service (receipted), if used. But you cannot insure the presumptive value—what you think it might bring you as a literary property.

But a safety measure that you can take to provide a better chance for it to reach its destination is to send it by certified mail—return receipt requested. This will require an extra charge, but you will receive a return-receipt card signed by someone at the publishing company acknowledging receipt of the package.

For less cost, you can enclose a self-addressed postcard and a note requesting the date of receipt by the editor, who can mark the information on it and put it in the mail.

Always check out postal rates for domestic and foreign mailings, because these are changed often.

Look into special rates by the pound or partial pound.

A letter can travel with the manuscript at a first class rate while the package goes for less.

If you enclose a letter in a package that is going by other than first class mail, you must write "Letter Enclosed" on the outside of the package and add first class postage for the letter.

You might find it convenient to obtain rubber stamps that say "First Class Mail" and "Do Not Bend," so you can put these statements on both sides of your envelopes (going both ways). However, you can also use a felt pen or crayon for this.

If you submit manuscripts to publications outside the United States, do not enclose return postage. U.S. stamps cannot be used. You must either enclose international return coupons (obtainable at your local post office), or—for less cost—a postal money order to the publisher for the foreign equivalent of the required return postage.

Make a note of every manuscript you send off.

Your Submission Should Be Recorded

A record book—or at least a sheet of paper or cards—should be used to note pertinent information about your submissions: title, date sent; and magazine, anthologist, or book publishing company to which it was sent. It would be useful also to list in a remarks section such information as whether or not a latest submission is a revision and any personal comments from editors.

After you have a good number of manuscripts circulating, this record will come in handy as a useful reference. It will help you avoid submitting work to editors to which it has already gone. At a glance you'll know your writing score: the number of manuscripts out, for how long (in case you might want to query), the number sold, etc.

Carbon copies of your manuscripts should be stored for easy reference, with duplicates of any covering letters. They can be put in file folders (along with your preliminary drafts) and placed in a metal filing cabinet, less expensive cardboard filing cabinet, or simply in cardboard cartons measuring about thirteen inches in width.

Despending on what is best for you, your folders can be filed in alphabetical order or in the order written.

Your Manuscript Has Been Sent Off—Now What?

Get to work on the next one!

You'll eventually know how you made out, so don't pace the floor and imagine the best or worst results. Use that energy at the typewriter to develop your writing abilities. Keep those stories coming. Practice the craft—and produce at the same time.

Don't be discouraged if your submission is rejected. Sometimes it takes months—even years—for a story to find the right editor.

Think about this. Suppose a story that you wrote traveled back and forth to editors over a period of several months, or even a year, and during that time all you could think about was that submitted manuscript, no other. Then, suppose you finally sold that story. All that time that you thought solely about the manuscript that was out of your hands was wasted as far as your writing goes. During that time you might have been productive!

Salable stories are not always purchased the first time out.

16

The Publishers' Responses

Rejections

When that familiar brown envelope returns after all of your hoping, don't sulk, become depressed, or get angry. Just put the contents into another envelope and ship it out the same day to the editor you've listed as next in line.

If, however, on rereading it you can see where improvement is possible, make those changes and send out the revision.

Be undaunted in your goal to publish this and new manuscripts.

If you stick to your writing with determination, in time you will have many submissions circulating, and the postman may bring you—in return for one of your manila envelopes—a letter from an editor with good news.

The professional way to be a writer is to write. No writer, even those who are established, ever had an easy time of it—with no disappointments. They've all had their share of rejection slips. The writer's life has its peaks and valleys. So why should it be any different for you?

You just have to ignore the failures. And you have to pay your dues.

If you can survive these frustrations—as the pros do—you, too, can see your work in print. And receive those checks in the mail.

What Is a Normal Manuscript Response Time?

Magazine and Anthologies

In some instances market notices will supply you with this information. Most magazines will answer you in perhaps a few days to a couple of weeks. You might consider six to eight weeks a reasonable time for your manuscript to be considered by magazine or anthology editors. After that time, you have every right to query, which you should do politely.

Book Publishers

Two or three months is a reasonable time for a reply on a novel submission. Even as short a manuscript as three chapters and an outline—or less—may have to be read by several people before a decision can be made.

A full novel manuscript may take as long as six months. Of course, if it was sent on invitation as the result of a query, it might be read in a comparatively short time.

A book sent in "cold," without a preliminary query, could have a year's wait.

This will give you a general idea of waiting time. However, in the final analysis, book publishers have no "normal" reporting time.

Inquiring About Your Manuscript

Following a wait of reasonable length, send the editor a note giving the title of your manuscript, the date it was sent, and any other related facts. Ask if it was received and offer to send another if it wasn't. You might, as a courtesy and convenience, include a self-addressed postcard. This might hasten a response. If the ms wasn't received, type another and submit it. (This should exemplify the importance of making a copy for yourself. If you didn't and it was lost, you'll have to start the piece all over again from scratch.)

If no reply is given in ten days to two weeks, inquire again, mentioning your first inquiry. You'll probably receive an answer this time—and it might even be your manuscript. It could be returned with no explanation, an apologetic note, or perhaps an irritating comment informing you that it had been slated for publication but since you were so anxious to have it back—here it is. Should you ever receive one of these highly uncommon responses, don't believe it. No self-respecting editor would treat a writer that way. You would have been advised of the status of your manuscript or at least have received a courteous reply to your query asking if your work could be held for further consideration.

If you do hear from an editor asking if your manuscript can be held longer, you should definitely allow it.

How much time should you give this editor?

Try to get a commitment. If you can't, three to six months is not unreasonable, considering that magazines and book publishers plan their schedules far in advance. But after that time is up, inquire as to the status of your submission.

In you are unable to get any response and an unreasonable amount of time has gone by, you may wish to telephone. Telephone inquiries about manuscripts are not exactly welcomed by editors because of disruption of schedules, so use it only if all other efforts fail. You will no doubt, however, be given a reason for the holdup.

Should none of your efforts result in success, you will have no choice but to withdraw your manuscript. To do this, send a notice by certified mail. Your letter should note the title, subject, and date of submission of your manuscript. State that you have queried and the dates you did so and that, having received no response, you are respectfully retracting the offer of your work for publication. Inform the editor that you will be offering it elsewhere.

And point out the fact that you won't have to retype a copy—if the manuscript is returned.

Don't Send Your Rejected Manuscript Out Unexamined

Your manuscript has come back. You check your records to see which editor you noted to send it to next. All you have to do is prepare a mailing envelope and an SASE—almost.

First, check each page. An editorial suggestion, made with good intention, might have been penciled in somewhere.

Perhaps a coffee ring might mark a page, though it isn't too likely.

So, before you send your typescript off again, see that any marks are neatly removed. If they're not removable, retype those pages. But do it so that the darkness of the letters matches the type on the other pages. To do this, either adjust the typewriter key pressure or use your previous ribbon. Also, flatten out creases. You don't want the next editor to think that the manuscript has been submitted elsewhere many times before being sent there.

Rejected Manuscript—Unsalable?

The decision to turn down your story or novel is usually only one person's opinion. Perhaps it involves more than one—if it gets past the first reader.

It is not uncommon for an editor to find a writer's manuscript unpublishable and even to mention so—and *why*—in rejecting it. And neither is it unusual for the same piece subsequently to bring its author a letter of acceptance, a contract, or a check—along with praise from another editor.

Writing is a strange, unpredictable, and sometimes exhilarating profession. The writer never knows what tomorrow will bring—except that there will be interesting experiences.

If you're determined to publish, stick with your typewriter.

Interpreting the Rejection Slip

The most common rejection slip—among the many varieties— is the one that is printed. In many different ways these formal notes inform you that the editor receives many submissions and therefore cannot answer you personally. They tell you that the turndown does not imply a lack of merit in your work. It may also invite you to try again.

But what does it *really* mean?

It's anybody's guess.

Just take it at its face value. In the future, whenever you write something that you feel is suitable for that market, submit it.

Occasionally, you will hear from an editor who has gone to the trouble of printing up a special rejection slip that contains a checkoff list of reasons for the turndown. Those reasons which apply are marked. Although this is still a printed rejection slip, it is more inclined toward personal comment and should be appreciated. Obviously, the editor is concerned about new writers, and time and effort is being devoted to them. Unsolicited manuscripts are being read and thought about there. Sometimes, besides the listing of flaws, one comment refers to a backlog of manuscripts with a statement that the editor will not be buying material for a specified number of months. Should this be checked off, it means that the editor would like to see that same manuscript of yours again. You should, therefore, make a note in your folder for that manuscript—and a note on your calendar—to resubmit it. The editor was considerate enough not to want to tie up your manuscript for a lengthy period of time. It is not unusual for such a manuscript to be purchased a year or more after its original submission. And when you resubmit it, be sure to remind the editor about the original interest.

How many aspiring writers have been encouraged to continue battling obstacles in order to make it in the field as the result of receiving a printed rejection slip on which was handwritten a brief personal comment by an editor? Many, no doubt. It might just be a simple: "Sorry." Should you ever receive such a response, as stark as it may be, you should certainly feel encouraged. It doesn't happen that often. The editor has seen something of value in your writing. For some reason, however, it could not be used. Why? Here are a few possible reasons: It is similar to something recently published by the editor or by another editor in the field. Not enough space was available. A rewrite might have helped, but the editor just didn't have the time to aid you in redoing the piece.

Another comment might be "Not convincing" or a similar specific statement. Do not be discouraged by this. On the contrary, though the editor's criticism may seen somewhat painful to accept, it is obvious that professional qualities in your writing have stimulated a response suggesting that your work could be salable with some improvement.

Another written comment that shows up on printed rejection slips is: "Try us again." If you should ever receive such a response, be assured that it means exactly what it says. You're certainly almost on target for the editor's needs. And when you try again, be sure to remind the editor of the comment—perhaps with a thank-you note. And say that if this one isn't right, you'd appreciate knowing where it's off, that you'd be willing, on spec, to rewrite it.

Probably the bottom-of-the-barrel type rejection is the return of your manuscript without even a rejection slip enclosed—or, worse yet, your covering letter returned with it. Why this kind of return? Who knows? Perhaps the editor was busy that morning or had indigestion. There's no doubt that such a rejection can ruin your day, so don't let it. It's only one of the many disappointments that occur in the writing life, which can also be full of delights and surprises.

Just continue to pursue your goals. Keep those manuscripts coming out of your typewriter and circulating in the mail.

Finally, there is the nonrejection rejection. Your manuscript is returned unread—possibly in its original envelope, which is unopened and rubber-stamped. You're informed that your material has not been seen, that unsolicited manuscripts will not be considered. This is why you should first check the markets—in this book, s.f. newszines, writers' magazines, and writers' reference books. Still, it is possible that this fact may not be stated in a market report, or there might have been a recent change in policy.

Should you get back an unconsidered ms, you might view the situation optimistically—your enclosed SASE postage was not canceled and can be used again.

Publishers who will not consider unsolicited manuscripts use such sources as their regular authors or agents with whom they deal regularly.

There is a way into these publishers' offices for the newcomer, however, though it is not guaranteed. Write to their editors describing your background and proposed submission. If this sparks their interest, you manuscript will then be solicited.

The most promising rejection is the one by which an editor sends you a personal letter expressing interest in your manuscript and suggests that you rewrite it on spec. This is a potential sale, and if you follow instructions—and the chemistry (and your luck) is right—you'll have a sale.

Okay, so what does a rejection mean, then?

If you're determined to be a writer, it doesn't mean a thing!

PART IV: ACCEPTANCE AND BEYOND

17

Payment and Protection

You're Going to Be Published

Congratulations!

You've made your first sale. The amount of payment makes no difference. Your words have been bought and they'll see print. It's a great feeling knowing that an editor liked your writing enough to buy it for readers.

In the future, no matter how well you may be paid for your literary efforts, it will never surpass that thrilling moment you had the day you became a professional writer.

What Do Editors Pay?

Magazines and Anthologies

When you are notified that your manuscript has been accepted, the editor will usually also inform you of the payment offered. A magazine has a usual rate of payment. Anthology editors pay varying rates.

You will most likely be notified by letter or contract; however, it might even be by phone.

It will then be up to you to respond regarding acceptance of the offer.

Payment for stories can be by the word or by flat payment. Anthologists usually have a rate per word and royalties based on a pro rata share among the writers in the anthology and the editor. Payment by other anthologies may be a flat rate per story.

The rates for genre magazines are noted in the market chapters of this book. Facts about rates, which can change, as well as current needs and new and disappearing genre magazines, are constantly updated in the latest s.f. newszines and professional writer trade publications. The only current listing of nonseries anthologies is in either s.f. newszines or SFWA publications, where rates as well as other requirements are provided.

The rates for nongenre magazines are in the market lists in the writers' trade magazines and annuals, though some often turn up in the genre listings.

Novels

Notification of your acceptance by letter or phone should inform you about such financial facts as advance against royalty, percentages, and other details regarding author's payment. Or you will first have to accept the offer (by letter or the phone call) before you are sent a contract.

Specific procedures are followed by book publishers in regard to advances against royalty and payment schedules.

When Will You Be Paid?

Magazine and Anthology

Genre magazine editors will usually send you a contract, as

will anthologists. Payment can be made on acceptance or on or after publication.

The men's magazines that rank below the top slick ones will usually, when a story is about to be published, send an informal contract in the form of a brief letter, or when the piece appears they will send a check along with a notice of acceptance.

If you've sold to an anthology, payment will probably arrive shortly after you sign the contract. On publication you should receive a complimentary copy of the book.

Certain s.f. magazines put out anthologies for which reprint rights and payment may already have been agreed upon.

Novels

The terms of payment on a book will be determined by your contract, which covers advance against royalties and subsequent royalty payments, from which your advance is deducted. Included also are book club sales and income that may accrue from other rights and licenses, if applicable.

Some books are given one printing and, as a result, never earn back all of their royalty advance. As a result, that is all the payment that the author receives. This can occur with a first novel.

The contract should note when you are to receive your advance, which is usually less than a month after you send the publisher the signed contract. The total advance, though, might not be given at once; it may be divided into partial payments, depending on any work that your book may need. It might bring you half on signing and the balance after you have turned in a completed manuscript to the satisfaction of the publisher. Another method of payment might be in thirds, with the last installment paid on publication.

If you are represented by an agent, the publisher will send your contracts and checks to that person. After deduction of the 10 percent or other agreed-on portion, your literary representative will forward the balance to you.

Your wait will, of course, depend on the paying practices of your agent.

You Get Paid

The check arrives and it's beautiful. Although you'd like to cash it, you also want to look at it. Should you make a photocopy and frame it?

Whether you'd like to put a copy on your wall or not, you should at least make a duplicate of it—perhaps more than one—for your files. Prior to cashing it and seeing it for the last time, sign it and get a copy of both the front and the back.

Why?

Here are some reasons:

- You will have documentary proof of the sum paid to you. This can be put with your receipts and other income tax records.
- A copy of the back of the check, with your signature, will show that it was not (or was) rubber-stamped—and is, therefore, proof that you did not sign away rights other than those to which you and the publisher agreed.
- The check duplicate can accompany the copy of your sold manuscript in its folder along with other related papers such as your contract (if any) and a copy of the magazine—or a copy of its pages having your story, the names of the editorial staff, and the copyright notice.
- Most important, a copy of the check will give you information that you might need in the future: the publisher's bank, account name, addresses of both the bank and (usually) the publisher, and the account numbers. Should you ever have need to litigate in order to collect payment from the publisher, and you obtain a judgment, this will serve as a record of an accessible asset.

Nonpayment—What Action to Take

Magazines can come upon hard times—and just not pay you.

Often, when letters, phone calls, and any other attempts to collect money owed are unsuccessful, the next best step is to file a complaint against the publisher in Small Claims Court. However, this can be done only in the municipality in which the publisher has offices. In most cases it will be New York City.

If you do not live where the publisher is located, you will have to go there to file your complaint. Otherwise, to accomplish your goal, it will be necessary to follow out-of-state procedures.

To file a complaint, call the Small Claims Court in your municipality. Tell them what your problem is and they will advise you regarding how you should take action.

A modest filing fee is required, which can be recovered after you obtain a judgment.

There is a maximum sum allowable for each Small Claims Court. Any amount above that sum must be sought through an attorney.

Upon getting a judgment, you can learn from the court the procedure to follow for obtaining the money owed to you.

Novels and Anthologies

Any disputes with a book publisher or anthology editor will involve your contract. A novel will be contracted directly with the publisher. However, regarding an anthology, you may be seeking payment from either the publisher or the editor.

If you are a member of SFWA, you can ask them for advice and assistance.

If you have a literary representative, that person will handle such problems for you. If it should become necessary, however, for there to be litigation, you should consult an attorney familiar with the writing field. Usually, it is not necessary for such drastic action to be taken when there are disputes between the writer and the publisher.

Collecting Your Published Work

Magazines

You should obtain at least two copies or more of any published stories. Sometimes you will receive, on publication, a complimentary copy from the publisher.

There will be times when you will want to submit a published story to an editor to be considered for reprinting. If so, never send an original, only a photocopy. Copies of published work often get put aside and sometimes are never returned.

Anthologies

The anthology editor or publisher of your story will most likely send you a copy of the book upon its publication. Nevertheless, it would be wise to obtain at least one other copy.

Stories published in original anthologies or continuing series original anthologies are eligible for best-of-the-year and other reprint volumes. Although the best-of-the-year anthologies are usually the personal selections of the editors, it doesn't hurt to bring your story to the attention of those editors.

Novels

If you publish a novel, the publisher will send you several copies. You should circulate one or two for reading. There is always someone who wishes to borrow a copy to read. And there should be a copy for you to show around for either professional or personal purposes.

Protecting Your Copies

To preserve your published work, each item—whether a book or in a magazine—should be sealed in clear plastic wrap. This will protect the contents from dust and handling, as well as discoloration and deterioration that might result from oxidation, and provide you with mint-condition copies of your work in its original published form.

Can Your Submissions Be Plagiarized?

There is no doubt that the possibility of your work being stolen exists; however, it isn't too likely that this will happen.

Should you have fears that your unpublished manuscript

might be ripped off while it's in the magazine or book publisher's office, keep in mind that a reputable publisher has too much at risk to gamble in this way. And in the s.f. community, word gets around with surprising speed.

Why should a publisher (especially a magazine publisher, who deals with many writers) take a chance on losing both readers and writers through such petty theft? The publisher has a budget for the purchasing of manuscripts. It certainly wouldn't be good business to save a few dollars on a story and lose thousands by antagonizing and, as a result, turning away good writers—including new ones—who would never send their work in again for consideration. Such an act would be detrimental to the reputation of both the publisher and the editor.

There is a possiblity that a minor employee of a publisher—who has little to lose, plus the protection of anonymity—might filch an idea from a submitted manuscript. However, it is quite unlikely.

Nevertheless, if a person is unscrupulous and has access to manuscripts by known or unknown writers—whether published or not—anything is possible. Even after publication of your work, there is no guarantee against plagiarism. Claims and even lawsuits dealing with such incidents in the film and television industries have been publicized.

Generally, however, you should not be overly concerned about the stealing of your ideas or plagiarism of your work. Much mental and physical energy can be spent wastefully in pursuit of a negligible loss, when it could be used for writing.

18

Literary Representation

Having an agent can be an advantage to a beginning writer. Ironically, however, finding one who is willing to represent someone new is difficult because an agent has overhead expenses that must be met through authors' commissions. Besides the time spent reading manuscripts and dealing with editors, there are postage, lunch tabs, and other related costs. And although the agent's stable of writers may well be established, perhaps even with some well-knowns, that doesn't assure that the works these writers produce will sell. For a new and unknown writer there is even less chance.

Still, there's always the possibility that if you try for representation, you might get it. If you do succeed at getting yourself an agent, what advantages might you expect?

You can no doubt get much better terms on a book than you might otherwise have obtained. It is quite likely that, having an agent, you will be offered an "agent's" contract from a publisher—one in which clauses found objectionable by agents have been removed. In addition, your agent, based on experience in the literary field, will delete or add certain phrases and dates. However, do not expect too much in the way of additional advance monies or percentages because, after all, you are a beginner with no track record to speak of.

An agent will most likely be better able than you to sell your next book.

Should your book do well, this and perhaps magazine publication might provide a solid basis for your agent to convince an editor during a luncheon meeting that you should be contacted to write a book on a subject in which that editor is interested. However, a publisher will most likely be inclined to take that sort of chance on a well-published and experienced writer instead of you.

In addition to dealing with your publisher, an agent can also negotiate in areas in which you have no contracts or expertise, such as film, television licensing, book club and foreign sales. A literary representative can phone an editor at a magazine or an anthology editor, or get your manuscript past the first readers or assistant editors at a publishing company and have it considered by the top editor—possibly even the publisher. And an agent can put your story through to magazines that are "closed" (do not read unsolicited manuscripts), and the slicks, which pay the best rates.

A good agent, then, can have your work seen by the right people.

The acceleration of your career can usually occur only after you've established basic credits in publication with stories or books.

The only way an agent can earn a substantial return through commissions (10 percent or more) is by representing authors who produce manuscripts that sell.

The "gentlemen's agreement" of 10 percent is being increased by some agents; so far, fortunately for the writers, there are few. Some, however, are large agencies.

Another advantage of representation is that the agent is able to obtain market information just about as soon as it becomes available, as well as publishing news regarding such situations as the emergence of a new magazine or book publisher. In addition, publishers who might want a particular type of story or book will often contact an agent rather than a writer.

Agents are not editors. They may suggest direction on a rewrite for a particular publisher. However, this would be an obligation to their clients only.

Certain agents will look at anyone's writing—but for a fee. Some of these fee-charging agencies are large and well known within the genre. However, most agents—if they consent to read your work—will not charge a fee. You may or may not want to go the route of the fee.

There are also companies and individuals who are not agents but represent themselves as literary services or consultants. They will revise (edit and rewrite) your work. For this, the fee can be quite high. You should, therefore, be aware before availing yourself of their service that it involves a single manuscript and that there will be no effort on their part to sell it. You would pay for advice but not representation. An agent's income is from a percentage of manuscript sales; the consultant's income comes from fees.

Some agents have contracts with their clients; others do not. If you are offered a contract, read it carefully before signing. You may want to consult SFWA, one of its members, or another writer's organization regarding not only the contract but the agent's reputation. An attorney who is knowledgeable about literary properties, copyright, and other aspects of the writing profession might be worth consulting, although this kind of specialist is even more difficult to find than an interested agent.

How do you go about finding an agent?

Well-published writers, when asked this question, will very seriously refer you to the *Yellow Pages*, suggesting that you start calling the names listed under literary agents. They mean, of course, the New York City (Manhattan) phone directory, because that is where most agents are concentrated.

A major advantage of the telephone inquiry is that you can cover a lot of ground quickly and possibly zero in very quickly on someone who will be interested in representing you. On the other hand, it can be an expensive search.

You can write to organizations that represent agents for their lists of members and their addresses. They are:

> The Society of Authors' Representatives, Inc.
> P.O. Box 650
> Old Chelsea Station
> New York, NY 10133

The Society's brochure of agents also includes a section entitled "The Literary Agent," which contains important information for writers.

> Independent Literary Agents Association
> P.O. Box 5247, FDR Station
> New York, NY 10150

Material may be obtained free from either organization by sending a request with an SASE.

Names and addresses of agents may also be found in the writers' annual books; occasionally a writer's magazine will run a list.

If you are a member of SFWA, you will have a directory of names and addresses of members and their agents; these are cross-indexed.

You can ask s.f. writers about their agents or for recommendations, whether or not you are a member of SFWA. With a small, selected list of possibilities, it might be worthwhile to use the telephone.

With hard work and good fortune—even without significant publishing credits—you may just find an agent interested in handling your work. But a way to obtain representation by a big name or any agency is by giving them a book contract to handle for you. In other words, *you* will have to sell that first novel. Then, with the still unsigned contract, telephone or write—and you should certainly spark interest.

If you are represented by an agent, you will not usually be given details about your rejections. Agents are aware that writers can be easily discouraged. And they are also too busy to provide infinite details to their clients. So, during the time that your short stories or novels are being sent from one publisher to another, you may not be told about their status. If you are affected by turndowns, this can benefit you. However, if you feel that knowing why your work is being rejected would help you, such an arrangement might be a disadvantage—unless you occasionally request information about your literary progress. However, on the other hand, where on your own you might get only a cold, printed rejection slip, an agent might not only get comments on your work, but a request for a rewrite as well.

Let's assume that it should suddenly occur to you—as the result of reading a market notice or even on a hunch—to send a particular manuscript off to a specific editor as soon as possible. Without an agent you can follow your inclinations, but with an agent this might not be possible.

There are established writers who, though they are represented, use their agents only to close deals to the best advantage—after they themselves have marketed their own manuscripts.

Is it necessary to have an agent?

No. Many writers handle their own manuscript sales—from those who have begun to sell, to others who are well established. They all receive 100 percent of the manuscript sale amounts.

Opting for literary representation is up to you. However, if you decide to go with an agent, it's the agent's choice, too.

19
Legal and Financial Matters

Income Tax Deductions for the Writer

You are legally entitled to literary tax deductions if you are a writer. It is important, therefore, that you keep exact records of what you spend for office equipment and stationery supplies (though your office may be in your own home or apartment), postage, and other related costs.

Also included among a writers' expenses are books and magazines that are directly related to the work.

The law allows deductions of a certain percentage of your mortgage principal, interest and real estate taxes, or rent, as well as of the cost of your utilities.

The Internal Revenue Service can provide you with information regarding tax regulations that are applicable to your situation. Should there be an income tax in the state of your residence, you should also look into those regulations.

An accountant who knows about tax matters related to

writers may in the long run prove quite beneficial to you financially despite the asked-for fee.

Copyright

On January 1, 1978, the new Copyright Law became effective. The basic term of copyright is for the life of the writer plus fifty years. According to Copyright Law, "A work is 'created' when it is fixed in a copy or phonorecord for the first time. . . ." The law also defines "copies." This means that your writing is copyrighted from the moment it is put in some form other than your silent thoughts—whether it is written by hand, typed, put into a word processor (or computer), or recorded by any means yet to be developed.

When a work is published and registered, the copyright belongs to the person (or corporate entity) whose name appears on the registration as the owner of the copyright.

The term of life plus fifty years after death is applicable if the work is copyrighted in your own name. However, if you use a pen name and the pen name is that of the registered owner, the copyright term is seventy-five years from the year of first publication or one hundred years from the year of its creation, whichever is the shorter period of time. If you reveal your true identity to the Copyright Office before the term expires, the term will revert to life plus fifty years.

Should you collaborate with one or more persons, the life-plus-fifty-years is counted from the date of death of the last surviving collaborator.

Three components comprise the notice of copyright: (1) the word *Copyright,* abbreviation *Copr.,* and/or the symbol ©; (2) the creation (or publication) year; and (3) the name of the copyright owner. An example would be: ©1982 Jane Doe.

You might want to put a copyright notice on your manuscript before submitting it. On a short work this could go on the first page under your name and address or at the bottom.

You might also specifically request in your covering letter that the copyright be in your name should the manuscript be accepted for publication.

A book publisher will usually do the registration work, in your name, for you.

If you are fearful of your unpublished manuscript being plagiarized (an infringement of copyright) you might want to register it before submission to any publisher.

You can obtain free literature regarding the many aspects of the Copyright Law, plus appropriate copyright forms, from the Copyright Office.

For a $10 fee you can register your work and obtain a copyright whether the manuscript is published or unpublished. Write to the Copyright Office for this information and to obtain the application forms you require:

Copyright Office
Library of Congress
Washington, DC 20559

Many rights are protected by copyright. When your manuscript is accepted to be published, certain of them are granted by you.

Magazines purchase first publication rights, known as first serial rights. First North American serial rights refer to publication in the United States and Canada. Some magazines may also purchase foreign rights.

Certain s.f. genre magazines issue reprint anthologies, and these magazines may have a reprint option in their contract giving them the right for a specific payment to reprint your story first. Should your published story be accepted for inclusion in a reprint anthology, such as best-of-the-year, you may have to obtain permission to have it reprinted.

Some magazines will purchase all rights, which include first and subsequent publications, usually for no additional payment to the writer.

Anthology contracts will contain the granting of any or all of the same rights as magazines, but some may be on a royalty basis, as a book contract, and may also retain certain subsidiary rights.

Unless specifically stated, once the story is published you own the reprint rights.

Book contracts are different. The author grants certain rights to the publisher in addition to the right of publication. The publisher may also share the profits the author might realize from other rights known as *subsidiary rights,* such as from sales to book clubs or movies covered under the copyright. The percentage of this share varies according to the publisher and is negotiable. However, these subsidiary rights of the author (such as dramatic rights, for example), protected by copyright, should not be granted in their entirety to a publisher. Nor should an author share with a publisher more than 50 percent of the profits realized from any of these subsidiary rights mentioned in the contract. And the copyright should be in your name only (or with your collaborator) and not shared with the publisher.

However, there is a form of contract by which you do not own the copyright to your work, known as *work for hire.* This phrase, *work for hire* (referred to in the copyright application) can represent either of two situations: that you are an employee receiving a salary or that you have been commissioned specifically to write the work, such as the novelization of a movie. There are publishers who will use this form of contract as a condition of sale, so you must read any contract—magazine, anthology, or book—very carefully. Whether or not you agree to sign such a contract is up to you.

Alternative Methods of Protecting Your Work

A way to assure ownership of a literary property that has been recommended through the years is for you to mail yourself a copy of your manuscript, which will show a stamped postal date, and not open the envelope. Then, should a controversy occur, the envelope can be opened under the proper conditions to produce legal proof.

Another method of proof of ownership is to send a copy to The Writers Guild of America Manuscript Registration Service. Certain materials can be left on deposit for ten years or longer. Fees differ at each of their coast offices with the basic cost for nonmembers at $10 (West) and $15 (East).

For further information, send an SASE to:

Writers Guild of America, East   Writers Guild of America, West
555 W. 57th St.   8955 Beverly Blvd.
New York, NY 10019   Los Angeles, CA 90048

Contracts

If you can't understand a contract, find someone who can. This is especially important if you have a book contract. If you are a member of SFWA, you can ask that organization for assistance or perhaps request it of an experienced member. Or, as previously suggested, you could get an agent—especially for a book contract. There are many aspects of book contracts in addition to the granting of rights. You might be offered a contract that is more favorable to the publisher; the degree of that advantage varies among publishers. A current development in the literary field is that, due to inflation, royalty percentages for the author are being lowered. Because of rising publication costs, other items in the contract may also be changed. Some contracts may have a clause requiring you to submit your next novel manuscript (or next two) to the publisher for consideration before submitting it elsewhere. This clause could contain a hidden time period (which, by omission, could be limitless) regarding how long the publisher has to look at this future manuscript before accepting or rejecting it; or, if accepted, what length of time there will be between the acceptance, publication, and distribution by the publisher. There are many hidden items of which you may not be aware. Thus, although you may feel capable of understanding a contract, in reality many items that work to your disadvantage could very well get by you due to your lack of experience in or knowledge about the literary field.

20
Science Fiction Markets

Magazine Markets

Two types of professional genre magazines are included in the following list—those devoted to the fiction of s.f. and one for the reader who is interested in science fiction. The latter are an acknowledgment by magazine publishers of the existence of the s.f. community and the fact that the fans and readers are interested in more regarding the genre than just its fiction. Other magazines are also listed, because they either have published s.f. or are interested in seeing s.f. stories.

Fanzines (those that pay, in money or issues, for fiction) and games magazines are not listed because they are available by subscription only and/or are not available to the general public at newsstands. A listing of these fanzines and games magazines can be found in the newszine market reports and in a yearly s.f. market booklet, *Othergates,* available for $5 from:

Unique Graphics
1025 55th St.
Oakland, CA 94608

Some of these fanzines have very small circulations. You may want to see a sample copy before submitting material.

As for the men's magazines other than those listed below, check them out at the newsstands to see which are currently in existence and if they publish s.f. Before you submit a manuscript to any magazine that appears to be for s.f. readers, check it out at the newsstands to be sure that it publishes fiction. Many of these types of magazines are nonfiction only. Other magazines (primarily the women's slicks) are not listed in this guide because, even though they may publish s.f., they are interested only in "name" authors or are not open to unsolicited manuscripts.

As for other markets not listed here, hundreds of other specialized subject, technical, trade, and professional magazines, journals, and house organs are listed in the writers' annual books. Although the vast majority of these are nonfiction only, a few publish fiction and may be interested in science fiction. Some of the magazines publish poetry. A large poetry market is also covered by these writers' annual books.

As for the two mystery magazines listed, you should keep in mind that, though they are interested primarily in mystery, they occasionally publish mixed-genre fiction (s.f.–mystery). Rules of the mystery genre that must be followed may be found in *Writing Mysteries That Sell*, by Harvey L. Bilker and Audrey L. Bilker (Contemporary Books, 1982).

Genre Magazines

AMAZING/FANTASTIC
P.O. Box 692
Scottsdale, AZ 85252
Editor: Elinor Mavor
Issued: Bimonthly; digest size.
Contents per issue: Seven to nine original short stories (including short-shorts), occasional short story reprints; opinion articles; science fact article; poetry (as many as five poems per issue); book reviews; letters; backgrounds of each fiction writer; sometimes an excerpt from a new novel; illustrations.

Requirements: All s.f. and fantasy categories; no sword & sorcery; only very special stories with something different to say; shorter fiction preferred, lengths up to 12,000 words.
Rates: 1¢ to 2¢ per word; payment on publication.
Contract: One-time world rights.

ANALOG SCIENCE FICTION/SCIENCE FACT
380 Lexington Ave.
New York, NY 10017
Editor: Stanley Schmidt
Issued: Thirteen times annually; digest size.
Contents per issue: Four to six short stories (usually one short-short); one or two novelettes, a novella, or a serialization of a new s.f. novel; science fact article; opinion article; short biography (usually illustrated with a photograph) of one of the writers in that particular issue; book reviews; calendar of conventions; letters; editorials by the editor or a guest editor; illustrations for each work. All fiction is original, except for novel serializations.
Requirements: Prefers hard s.f., occasionally softened, and some soft s.f. Any fiction touching the fantasy category always contains elements of hard or soft s.f. Occasionally publishes alternate history. There is usually a humorous story in each issue. Published under several names since its inception in 1930, this is the oldest s.f. magazine still in existence.
Rates: 5.75¢ per word up to 7,500 words; 4.3¢ per word, 7,500 to 12,500 words; 3.5¢ per word for fiction over 12,500 words. Pays more for regular contributors. Pays on acceptance.
Contract: All serial rights, nonexclusive foreign serial rights, reprint option.
Note: Issues reprint anthologies. Publisher, Davis Publications, Inc., also publishes *IASFM*.

ISAAC ASIMOV'S SCIENCE FICTION MAGAZINE
380 Lexington Ave.
New York, NY 10017
Editor: Kathleen Maloney
Issued: Thirteen times annually; digest size.

Contents per issue: Five or six original short stories (some short-shorts); three poems; editorial by Asimov; book reviews; opinion articles; articles about science; convention listing; puzzle; letters; illustrations for each work.

Requirements: Hard and soft s.f. and a bit of s.f./fantasy; usually has a humorous story or two each issue, some of which are puns. Nothing longer than 20,000 words.

Rates: 5.75¢ per word to 7,500 words; 4.3¢ per word up to 12,500 words; 3.5¢ per word over 12,500 words. Pays more for regular contributors. Pays on acceptance.

Contract: First North American serial rights, foreign serial rights, reprint option.

Note: Issues reprint anthologies. Publisher, Davis Publications, Inc., also publishes *Analog*.

THE MAGAZINE OF FANTASY & SCIENCE FICTION
P.O. Box 56
Cornwall, CT 06753
Editor: Edward L. Ferman
Issued: Monthly; digest size.
Contents per issue: Five or six short stories; two or three novelettes and/or one novella; book reviews; dramatic reviews; two cartoons; science fact article by Asimov; occasionally has letters; some issues have either an acrostic puzzle or a contest. The only illustration is the cover. All fiction is original.
Requirements: This magazine publishes the highest quality of s.f. and fantasy literature. All s.f. and fantasy categories.
Rates: 3¢ to 4¢ per word. Pays on acceptance.
Contract: First North American rights, first foreign rights, reprint option.
Note: Issues reprint anthologies.

ROD SERLING'S THE TWILIGHT ZONE MAGAZINE
800 Second Ave.
New York, NY 10017
Editor: T.E.D. Klein
Issued: Monthly.

Contents per issue: Seven to nine stories (some short-shorts) of original fiction with an occasional reprint; book reviews; dramatic reviews; background information on writers whose works appear in each issue; illustrations. The rest of the articles, items, and fiction is this magazine are devoted to the TV show, "Twilight Zone." There is a synopsis of individual shows, plus an entire show script.

Requirements: If you have seen any of the TV shows, you will be familiar with the type of fiction required by this magazine. Also, the show scripts and the synopsis of individual shows in each issue are an excellent guide. Requires the human (or alien) factor to be stressed, for horror, supernatural, suspense, fantasy/s.f./horror combinations—the more spine-tingling types of s.f. stories.

Rates: $150 and up.

Note: This magazine has a short story contest "for the best work of supernatural horror, fantasy, or suspense by a previously unpublished writer." Cash prizes, plus winning stories will be published. Check magazine for deadline date and other details for each contest.

Magazine for S.F. Readers

OMNI
909 Third Ave.
New York, NY 10022
Fiction Editor: Ellen Datlow
Issued: Monthly.
Contents per issue: Two pieces of fiction, original or translation. The rest of the magazine is devoted to other aspects of the genre, including art and nonfiction articles of interest to s.f. readers. There are also book and dramatic reviews and background information on all contributors in each issue.
Requirements: Quality s.f. and fantasy; no sword & sorcery or poetry; lengths up to 7,500 words.
Rates: $1,250 to $2,000, with contract.
Note: Issues reprint anthologies.

Men's Magazines

CAVALIER
2355 Salzedo St.
Coral Gables, FL 33134
Editor: Nye Willden
Requirements: Any s.f., 2,500 to 3,500 words in length.
Rates: Up to $250.

GALLERY
800 Second Ave.
New York, NY 10017
Editorial Director: Eric Protter
Requirements: Any s.f., especially adventure stories, 500 to 3,000 words in length.
Rates: From $250.

GENESIS MAGAZINE
770 Lexington Ave.
New York, NY 10021
Editor: Joseph Kelleher
Requirements: Quality s.f., with upbeat endings, up to 3,000 words in length.

OUI MAGAZINE
300 W. 43rd St.
New York, NY 10036
Fiction Editor: Pierce Wayne
Requirements: S.f. and fantasy, for men, up to 5,000 words in length.
Rates: $500 and up.

PENTHOUSE
909 Third Ave.
New York, NY 10022
Fiction Editor: Kathryn Green
Requirements: Any s.f., 3,500 to 6,000 words in length.
Rates: $750 and up.

PLAYBOY
919 N. Michigan Ave.
Chicago, IL 60611
Fiction Editor: Alice K. Turner
Requirements: Publishes up to five s.f. stories per year, usually but not always by well-known s.f. writers. Subject matter is unrestricted; lengths up to 7,500 words.
Rates: $2,000 and up.

SWANK
888 Seventh Ave.
New York, NY 10019
Fiction Editor: Dave Trilby
Requirements: S.f. or s.f./fantasy, but science fiction is stressed; lengths to 3,000 words.
Rates: $300 and up.

Mystery Magazines

ALFRED HITCHCOCK'S MYSTERY MAGAZINE
Editor: Cathleen Jordan
and/or
ELLERY QUEEN'S MYSTERY MAGAZINE
380 Lexington Ave.
New York, NY 10017
Editor: Eleanor Sullivan
Requirements: Both magazines occasionally publish a mixed-genre story; however, the mystery is stressed over s.f. and the story must follow the rules of the mystery genre and the story requirements for each magazine. The publisher of these magazines also publishes *Analog* and *IASFM*. Lengths range from short-shorts of 1,000 words up to fiction of 12,000 words.
Rates: 3¢ to 8¢ per word; contract.
Note: Both magazines have regular reprint anthologies.

Continuing Series Original Anthologies

Only the continuing series original anthologies are listed here.

Market information for one-time original anthologies can be found in the newszines.

Anthologies are usually originated by their editor (anthologist), though some anthologies originate with the publishing house and belong to that house. The freelance anthologist can place the book with any publisher and can usually change publishers. The anthologist has a contract with the publisher. The individual writers have their contracts with the anthologist, not the publisher, though the publisher is usually mentioned in that contract.

Anthologists will usually offer an advance, a specific cents-per-word amount, against a pro rata share of the royalties, with the editor taking up to 50 percent of this share. Some anthologists may offer a flat fee, but this is usually for a reprint anthology. The anthologist may pay the writer directly from personal funds (or funds advanced by the publisher), or the publisher may pay the writer directly.

Anthologists have different payment rates, depending on each individual book contract with the publisher, and payment varies widely.

Anthologists also have deadlines beyond which they will *not* consider material for a particular book. Before submitting any manuscript, inquire as to whether the anthologist is accepting any material and what the submission deadline is—and be sure to enclose an SASE. However, the most up-to-date information can be found in the newszines.

The anthologies below are listed by the name of the anthologist, not the name of the anthology. This is because very often these anthologists put out more than one series, one-time original anthologies, limited series, or a continuing series.

Anthologies

TERRY CARR, EDITOR
1103 Broadway Terrace
Oakland, CA 94611
Anthology: Universe

CHARLES L. GRANT, EDITOR
Box H
Budd Lake, NY 07828
Anthology: Shadows—quiet horror stories.

J. E. POURNELLE & ASSOC.
c/o John F. Carr, Associate Editor
12051 Laurel Terrace
Studio City, CA 91604
Anthologies: Miscellaneous one-time anthologies.

MARTA RANDALL, EDITOR
P.O. Box 13243
Station E
Oakland, CA 94661
Anthologies: *New Dimensions*

JESSICA AMANDA SALMONSON, EDITOR
2127 S. 254th Place
Kent, WA 98031
Anthologies: Miscellaneous one-time or limited series, fantasy only.

Book Markets

The harsh reality of the book market is that very few publishers will accept unsolicited manuscripts. However, most will definitely consider a query letter with an outline, or three chapters and an outline. It is on this basis that the book market is presented here—not just as a listing of those houses that publish s.f. or fantasy or those that say they are interested in the genre, but only those houses that are open to some form of submission. Although most of the markets listed below prefer to deal only through agents, they *are* interested in beginning writers or first-time novelists.

Advances and royalties are not listed because they all, without exception, vary and are open to negotiation. Advances can run from a low of $1,000 up. First-time novelists naturally will get a low advance. Royalties are in a state of change, primarily due to inflation. The standard royalty for hardcovers is usually said to be 10 percent on the first 5,000 copies, 12½ percent on the next 5,000, and 15 percent thereafter (the percentage being based on the retail sales price of the book); with paperbacks the percentage can be 4 percent to 6 percent on the first 150,000, and 6 percent to 8 percent thereafter. If a publisher is interested in your work, you can always bargain or get an agent to do your bargaining for you.

Unless specifically noted, publishers will consider photocopies, providing they are clear and easily readable. If a house is interested in your manuscript, you may be requested to submit the original. However, one form of manuscript copy that is definitely not appreciated by editors is the kind produced by means of a word processor that prints its letters in "dots," whether the original or a photocopy. If at all possible, avoid using this sort of word processor.

Most publishers do not accept multiple submissions. Those that do are so noted here. However, if your manuscript is a multiple submission, *always* inform the publisher of that fact.

The number of titles published (per month or per year) are for original novels only. They do not include reprints (if any), anthologies, or collections.

Only three editors are noted, because their names are associated with their book imprints. Editors can change jobs, so it is best to address your manuscript to the science fiction (or fantasy) editor, if one is indicated in the listing. Otherwise, write to the "editor."

Before mailing anything, always check to be sure you have included an SASE—even for a query and outline.

Market conditions can change quite suddenly, so always check

the latest market report information before submitting manuscripts.

Books

ACE BOOKS
Science Fiction Editor
51 Madison Ave.
New York, NY 10010
(212) 689-9200
Titles: Four to six per month, paperback.
Submit: Three to five chapters with outline.
Word length: 50,000 minimum.
Categories: All s.f. and fantasy; does not want UFO speculation
à la Von Daniken.

ARBOR HOUSE PUBLISHING CO.
235 E. 45th St.
New York, NY 10017
(212) 599-3131
Submit: Query letter and outline.

ATHENEUM/ARGO BOOKS
597 Fifth Ave.
New York, NY 10017
(212) 486-2700
Titles: Three per year, hardcover, adult; five or six per year,
hardcover, young adult (ARGO).
Submit: Three chapters and outline.
Categories: All s.f. and fantasy; watch language, violence, and
sex in young adult fiction.

AVON BOOKS
959 Eighth Ave.
New York, NY 10019
(212) 262-5700
Titles: Paperback.

Submit: Three chapters and outline; will accept multiple submissions.
Categories: All s.f. and fantasy.

BANTAM BOOKS, INC.
Science Fiction Editor
666 Fifth Ave.
New York, NY 10019
(212) 756-6500
Titles: Paperback.
Submit: Query letter and outline.
Categories: All s.f. and fantasy.

BEAUFORT BOOKS, INC.
9 E. 40th St.
New York, NY 10016
(212) 685-8588
Submit: Query letter and outline.

BERKELEY PUBLISHING CORP.
Science Fiction Editor
200 Madison Ave.
New York, NY 10016
(212) 686-9820
Titles: Twelve to fifteen per year, paperback.
Submit: Query letter and outline; will accept multiple submissions.
Word length: 60,000 to 120,000.
Categories: All s.f. and fantasy; submit horror to BERKELEY/
JOVE.

CROWN PUBLISHERS, INC.
1 Park Ave.
New York, NY 10016
(212) 532-9200
Titles: Hardcover.

Submit: Either query letter and outline or three chapters and outline.
Categories: All s.f. and fantasy.

DAW BOOKS
Editor: Donald A. Wollheim
1633 Broadway
New York, NY 10019
(212) 397-8017
Titles: Four per month, paperback.
Submit: Entire manuscript or three chapters and outline.
Categories: All s.f. and fantasy; no occult or UFO speculation.

DEL REY BOOKS
Editor: Judy-Lynn Del Rey
201 E. 50th St.
New York, NY 10022
(212) 751-2600
Titles: Three per month, paperback.
Submit: Entire manuscript.
Word Length: 80,000 to 120,000.
Categories: All s.f. and fantasy; no UFO speculation.

DOUBLEDAY & CO., INC.
Science Fiction Editor
245 Park Ave.
New York, NY 10017
(212) 953-4561
Titles: Fourteen per year, hardcover, "Doubleday Science Fiction."
Submit: Three chapters and outline; wants only original manuscript.
Word length: 60,000 to 80,000.
Categories: All s.f. and fantasy

E. P. DUTTON PUBLISHING CO., INC.
2 Park Ave.
New York, NY 10016
(212) 725-1818
Submit: Query letter and outline or one or two chapters and outline.
Categories: All s.f. and fantasy.

FANTASY & SCIENCE FICTION/
CHARLES SCRIBNER'S SONS
Editor: Edward L. Ferman
P.O. Box 56
Cornwall, CT 06753
(203) 672-6376
Titles: Hardcover; "Charles Scribner's Sons, a Magazine of Fantasy & Science Fiction Book."
Submit: Prefers entire manuscript, but will look at three chapters (50 pages) and an outline.
Categories: All s.f. and fantasy, except no sword & sorcery or heroic fantasy.

FARRAR, STRAUS, & GIROUX, INC.
19 Union Sq.
New York, NY 10003
(212) 741-6900
Titles: Few per year, hardcover.
Submit: Query letter and outline.
Categories: All s.f. and fantasy; does not want overt violence or sex.

FAWCETT GOLD MEDAL
1515 Broadway
New York, NY 10036
(212) 975-7673
Titles: Three per year, paperback.
Submit: Query letter and outline; or telephone.
Word length: 60,000 to 120,000.
Categories: Occult, horror, adventure/action, space opera.

FAWCETT POPULAR LIBRARY
1515 Broadway
New York, NY 10036
(212) 975-7693
Titles: Paperback.
Submit: Query letter and outline.
Categories: All s.f. and fantasy, but only interested in young adult fiction.

HARMONY BOOKS
1 Park Ave.
New York, NY 10016
(212) 532-9200
Titles: Three per year (publishes hardcover, paperback, and trade).
Submit: Entire manuscript.
Word length: 40,000 minimum.
Categories: All s.f. and fantasy.

HARPER & ROW PUBLISHERS, INC.
Science Fiction Editor
10 E. 53rd St.
New York, NY 10022
(212) 593-7211
Titles: One or two per year, hardcover.
Submit: Query letter and outline.
Word length: 50,000 minimum.
Categories: Soft s.f. and fantasy.

HOLT, RINEHART & WINSTON
383 Madison Ave.
New York, NY 10017
(212) 688-9100
Titles: A few per year, hardcover.
Submit: Query letter and outline.
Categories: No horror, violence, or sex.

HOUGHTON MIFFLIN CO.
Science Fiction Editor
2 Park St.
Boston, MA 02107
(617) 725-5000
Titles: A few; hardcover.
Submit: Query letter and outline.
Word length: 50,000 minimum.
Categories: S.f. and fantasy; no occult or UFO speculation.

HOUGHTON MIFFLIN CHILDREN'S BOOK DIVISION
Science Fiction Editor
2 Park St.
Boston, MA 02107
(617) 725-5000
Titles: Hardcover.
Submit: Entire manuscript.
Word length: 25,000 minimum.
Categories: All s.f. and fantasy suitable for children, ages eight to twelve.

MACMILLAN PUBLISHING CO., INC.
866 Third Ave.
New York, NY 10022
(212) 935-2000
Titles: Hardcover.
Submit: Query letter and outline or three chapters and outline, but no more than a total of 100 pages.
Categories: All s.f. and fantasy.

NEW AMERICAN LIBRARY
1633 Broadway
New York, NY 10019
(212) 397-8000

Titles: Four to six per month; publishes paperback and hardcover; NAL, SIGNET, and MENTOR.
Submit: Three chapters and outline.
Word length: 60,000 to 80,000.
Categories: All s.f. and fantasy.

PHILOMEL BOOKS
200 Madison Ave.
New York, NY 10016
(212) 576-8900
Titles: One or two per year; young adult.
Submit: Query letter and outline.
Categories: All s.f. and fantasy, suitable for young adult, ages twelve and up; watch language, violence, and sex.

PLAYBOY PAPERBACKS
1633 Broadway
New York, NY 10019
(212) 245-9160
Titles: Twelve per year, paperback.
Submit: Query letter and outline.
Word length: 75,000 to 150,000.
Categories: All s.f. and fantasy.

G. P. PUTNAM'S SONS
200 Madison Ave.
New York, NY 10016
(212) 576-8900
Titles: Hardcover.
Submit: Query letter and outline; will accept multiple submissions.
Categories: All s.f. and fantasy.

ST. MARTIN'S PRESS
175 Fifth Ave.
New York, NY 10010
(212) 674-5151
Titles: Hardcover.
Submit: Query letter and outline.
Word length: 80,000 to 90,000.
Categories: All s.f. and fantasy.

STARBLAZE—THE DONNING CO. PUBLISHERS, INC.
Science Fiction Editor
5659 Virginia Beach Blvd.
Norfolk, VA 23502
(804) 461-8090
Titles: Hardcover.
Submit: Query letter and outline.
Categories: All s.f. and fantasy.

TAPLINGER PUBLISHING CO.
Science Fiction Editor
132 W. 22nd St.
New York, NY 10011
(212) 741-0801
Titles: Hardcover.
Submit: Query letter and outline or three chapters and outline.
Categories: No sword & sorcery, space opera, or horror; only wants very serious literature, not typical s.f. or fantasy. Publishes what other publishers are not doing; wants avant-garde and experimental fiction.

TIMESCAPE—POCKET BOOKS
Science Fiction Editor
1230 Ave. of the Americas
New York, NY 10020
(212) 246-2121

Titles: Four per month, paperback; hardcover only for established writers.
Submit: Entire manuscript.
Categories: All s.f. and fantasy.

TOR BOOKS—THOMAS DOHERTY ASSOCIATES
8 W. 36th St.
New York, NY 10018
(212) 564-0150
Titles: Two per month, paperback.
Submit: Three chapters and outline; mark on envelope whether s.f., fantasy, or occult.
Word length: 65,000 minimum.
Categories: All s.f. and fantasy.

TOWER PUBLICATIONS, INC.
2 Park Ave.
New York, NY 10016
(212) 679-7707
Titles: Paperbacks; also LEISURE BOOKS paperback.
Submit: Entire manuscript.
Word length: 60,000 minimum.
Categories: All s.f. and fantasy.

THE VIKING PRESS, INC., PUBLISHERS
625 Madison Ave.
New York, NY 10022
(212) 755-4330
Titles: Hardcover.
Submit: Three chapters and outline.
Word length: 50,000 minimum.
Categories: All s.f. and fantasy.

VINTAGE BOOKS
201 E. 50th St.
New York, NY 10022
(212) 751-2600
Titles: Hardcover.
Submit: Three chapters and outline.
Categories: Wants literary quality, socially oriented s.f.

ZEBRA BOOKS
21 E. 40th St.
New York, NY 10016
(212) 889-2299
Titles: Paperback.
Submit: Three chapters and outline.
Word length: 60,000 minimum.
Categories: Prefers sword & sorcery.

Index

A

Academe, 37, 43
Academy of Science Fiction,
    Fantasy and Horror Films,
    viii, 45
Ace Books, 141
Action. *See* Dialogue and action
Agents, 79, 113, 115, 119–23
*Alfred Hitchcock's Mystery
    Magazine,* 137
Algol Press, 68
Alien, viii
aliens, 3, 10, 11, 20
Alternate history
    definition, 4
    examples, 11
Alternate universes (worlds), 20
Amazine/Fantastic, 132, 133
American Booksellers
    Association, 68
*Analog Science Fiction/Science
    Fact,* 14, 63, 133, 134, 137
Anthropology, 4
Apollo astronauts, 7
Arbor House Publishing Co.,141
Archeology, 4

Art, s.f., 44
Artists, s.f., 44
Arts, 4
ASFA. *See* Association of SF
    Artists
Asimov, Isaac, 20, 35, 48
    three laws of robotics, 20
Association of SF Artists, 44
Astrology, 2, 4
Astronomy, 3
Astrophysics, 3
Atheling, William, Award, 65
Atheneum/Argo Books, 141
Avon Books, 141, 142
Awards, viii, 39, 45, 55, 61–66
    Atheling, William, Award, 65
    Balrog, 64
    British Fantasy Awards, 65
    BSFA Award, 65
    Campbell, John W., Award,
        63
    Campbell, John W., Memorial
        Award, 63, 64
    Derleth, August, Award, 66
    Ditmar, 65
    Gandalf, 63
    Grand Master (SFWA), 62

Grey Mouser, 65
Hugo, 39, 46, 62, 63
Jupiter, 49, 64
Nebula, 39, 48, 58, 59, 62, 81
Pilgrim, 49, 64
Rhysling, 39, 64, 65
World Fantasy Award, 63

B

Balrog, 64
Bantam Books, Inc., 142
Beaufort Books, Inc., 142
Berkeley Publishing Corp., 142
Berkeley/Jove, 142
Blurbs, 48
Bookstores, s.f., 39
Bowker, R. R., Co., 35
British Fantasy Awards, 65
British Fantasy Society, 66
British Fantasycon, 65
British Science Fiction
    Association, Ltd., 60
Brown, Charles N. (Charlie), 68,
    69
BSFA. *See* British Science
    Fiction Association, Ltd.
BSFA Award, 65
BSFA Easter Convention, 65
"Buck Rogers," 5
Bulletin, The, 59, 69

C

Campbell, John W., Award, 63
Campbell, John W., Memorial
    Award, 63, 64

Carr, Terry, 138
Cavalier, 136
Chemistry, 3
Clarion Science Fiction
    Workshop, 32
Clone, 3, 20
Collaborations, 33, 34
Community, science fiction. *See*
    Science fiction community
Conferences, 31, 32, 49
Conjecture, 6
Conventions, 37–39, 41, 42,
    44–46, 51–56, 62–65, 90
Cons. *See* Conventions
Copyright, 79, 126–28
    Office, 127
    work for hire, 128
Covering letters, 92, 93
Crown Publishers, Inc., 142, 143

D

Datlow, Ellen, 135
DAW Books, 143
Definitions, 2–11
    alternate history, 4
    conjecture, 6
    double-genre, 7
    fantasy, 4
    gothic horror, 5
    gothic science fiction, 6
    hard fantasy, 4
    hard s.f., 3
    heroic fantasy, 4, 5
    horror, 5
    mainstream s.f., 6
    mixed-genre, 6, 7
    science fiction, 2–4

soft s.f., 3, 4
space opera, 5
space Western, 6
speculative fiction, 5, 6
speculation, 5, 6
sword & sorcery, 4, 5
Del Rey Books, 143
Del Rey, Judy-Lynn, 143
Derleth, August, 5
  Award, 66
Dialogue and action, 30
Disclave, 51
Discovery, 16
Ditmar, 65
Doubleday & Co., Inc., 143
Double-genre, 1
  definition, 7
Down Under Fan Fund, 45
Dragons, 9, 10, 20
DUFF. *See* Down Under Fan
  Fund
Dutton, E. P., Publishing Co.,
  Inc., 144
Dystopias, 20

E

Ecology, 4
Economics, 4
Editors, 38, 39, 42, 43, 47–49,
  53, 73–75, 78, 81, 82, 85,
  86, 90, 91–93
Education in writing, an, 31, 32
*Ellery Queen's Mystery
  Magazine,* 137
Engineering, 3
  genetic (*see* Genetic engineering)
Entertainment, 4

ESP, 4, 20
Evolution, 4
Explanations, 25, 26
Extrapolation, 49
Extrasensory perception. *See*
  ESP
Extraterrestrials. *See* aliens

F

False science, 2
Fans (fandom), 37, 39, 41–46
  conventions, 51–56
  First Fandom (*see* First
    Fandom)
  origin of fandom, 41, 42
  social structure, 43
  typical, 43–45
*Fantasy & Science Fiction. See
  Magazine of Fantasy &
  Science Fiction, The*
Fantasy & Science
  Fiction/Charles Scribner's
  Sons, 144
*F&SF. See Magazine of Fantasy
  & Science Fiction, The*
Fantasy, 1
  definition, 4
  hard, 4
  heroic, 4, 5
  examples, 9
Fantasy Faire, 65
Fantasy/s.f., 1
Fanzines, 38, 41, 67, 131, 132
Farrar, Straus, & Giroux, Inc.,
  144
Faster-than-light, 2, 20
Fawcett Gold Medal, 144

Fawcett Popular Library, 145
Ferdinand Feghoot, 26
Ferman, Edward L., 134, 144
Fiawol, 51
First Fandom, 41
"Flash Gordon," 5
Fool-Con, 54, 64

G

Galactic empires, 20
Gallery, 136
Gandalf, 63
Genesis Magazine, 136
Genetic engineering, 3
Gernsback, Hugo, 62
Getting the science right, 22–24
GOH, 54
Gothic horror. *See* horror
Gothic s.f., 6, 7
Grand Master (SFWA), 62
Gothic s.f., 6, 7
Grant, Charles L., 139
Green, Kathryn, 136
Grey Mouser, 65
Guest of Honor. *See* GOH

H

Hard fantasy, 4
Hard s.f.
   definition, 3
   examples, 8, 9
Harmony Books, 145
Harper & Row Publishers, Inc.,
   145
Heinlein, Robert, 64

Heroic fantasy, 4, 5
History, 4
   alternate (*see* Alternate history)
Holt, Rinehart & Winston, 145
Horror, 1
   definition, 5
   Gothic horror, 5
   examples, 11
Houghton Mifflin Co., 146
Houghton Mifflin Children's
      Book Division, 146
Hucksters, 53
Hugo, 39, 46, 62, 63
Humanities, the, 4
Humor, 19, 26

I

*IASFM. See Isaac Asimov's
      Science Fiction Magazine*
Ideas, generating, 17–19
   development, 20–28
If only . . . , 17–19
If this goes on . . . , 17–19
Ifs, three, 17
   examples, 17–19
Income tax deductions, 125, 126
Incorrect science, 24, 25
Independent Literary Agents
      Association, 122
*Isaac Asimov's Science Fiction
      Magazine,* 14, 133, 134, 137

J

Japanese Science Fiction
      Writers, 66

Jordan, Cathleen, 137
Jupiter Award, 49, 64

K

Kelleher, Joseph, 136
Klein, T. E. D., 134
Kubla Kahn, 51

L

Language, 27
Legends, 4
Life forms, 3
"Literary Agent, The," 122
Literary Market Place, 35
LMP. See Literary Market Place
Locus, 67–70
Lovecraft, H. P., 63
Lunarians, 51

M

Macmillan Publishing Co., Inc.,
    146
*Magazine of Fantasy & Science
    Fiction, The,* 14, 35, 68, 134
Magic, 4
Mainstream s.f.
  definition, 6
  examples, 7, 8
Maloney, Kathleen, 133
Manuscript
  appearance, 77–80
  checking returned
      manuscripts, 104–7

fastening of, 87
format, 78–80
inquiring about delays, 102–4
length, 81, 82
protection of, 85, 115, 116
rejections, 101, 102
responses, 102–4
sending, 78, 95–98
submission records, 98
words, counting, 81–83
Markets, 131–50
  magazine, 131–37
  anthology, 137–39
  book, 139–50
Mathematics, 3
Mavor, Elinor, 132
Medical sciences, 3, 4
Mentor, 147
Meteorology, 3
Milford Science Fiction Writers'
    Conference, 31, 32
Mineralogy, 3
Mixed-genre
  definition, 6, 7
  examples, 11
Movies, s.f., viii, 1, 13, 14, 55
Multiple submissions, 85–87
Music, s.f. *See* Songs, s.f.
Mystery genre, 1, 6, 7, 11, 132
Mystery/s.f., 6, 11
Mythology, 4

N

NAL, 147
Nebula, 39, 48, 58, 59, 62, 81
Nebula Awards Anthology, 58
New American Library, 146, 147

New Dimensions, 139
New York Times, The, 16
Newszines, 38, 39, 67–70, 138
Nonpayment, 114, 115
Norwescon, 51
Nycon, 41

O

Omni, 16, 135
Organizations, s.f. writers, 57–60
Othergates, 131
Oui Magazine, 136
Outer space, 3

P

Parallel universes (worlds), 20
Pautz, Peter, 58
Payment, 111–14, 138, 140
Pen names, 80, 81
Penthouse, 136
Philcon, 51
Philomel Books, 147
Philosophy, 4
Photocopied submissions, 85–87
Physics, 3
Pilgrim, 49, 64
Plagiarism, 116, 117
Playboy, 137
Playboy Paperbacks, 147
Plotting, 20–22
Plotting ideas
    auto extras, 19
    baseball games, 18
    detached astronaut, 30
    England wins/1776, 4

future sports, 18
Hitler not born, 4
Karl Marx nonexistence, 4
"license to kill," 19
no news, 17
Roman Empire, 4
sample story line/all
    categories, 7–11
South wins Civil War, 4
thawed writer, 18, 19, 21–25, 31
Poe, Edgar Allan, 5
Poetry, 26, 27, 45, 64, 65
Politics, 4
Porter, Andrew (Andy), 68, 69
Pournelle, J. E., & Assoc., 139
Pros, the, 37, 42, 47–49, 52, 54,
    55, 61
Protection of work, 128, 129
Protter, Eric, 136
Psi, 4
Psychic powers, 4, 20
Psychology, 4
Publishers, 38, 39, 47–49, 53, 63,
    73, 74, 86, 90
Putnam's Sons, G. P., 147

Q

Queries, 89–93
    novel, 90, 91
    reply, 91, 92
    short story, 89, 90
Quest, 4

R

Randall, Marta, 139

Reality, 27, 28
References, general writing
  books, 33–35
  magazines, 24, 32
Religious beliefs, 4
Rhysling, 39, 64, 65
Robots, 3, 21
  laws, 20
*Rod Serling's The Twilight Zone
  Magazine,* 14, 134, 135
Roget's International Thesaurus,
  35
Royalties, 140

S

St. Martin's Press, 148
Salmonson, Jessica Amanda,
  139
Schmidt, Stanley, 133
Science Digest, 15
Science 82, 15, 16
Science fiction
  categories and examples, 2–11
  definitions (*see* definitions)
  hard (*see* hard s.f.)
  mainstream (*see* mainstream
    s.f.)
  soft (*see* soft s.f.)
Science Fiction Chronicle, 67–70
Science fiction community, ix, 1,
  37–70
  academe, 49
  awards, 61–66
  conventions, 51–56
  daydreams, 42, 43
  fans (fandom), 41–46
  pros, 47–49

publications, 67–70
publishers, editors, and
    writers, 47, 48
s.f. writers' organizations,
    57–60
social structure, 43
value of, 32–39
Science Fiction Poetry
    Association, 45, 64, 65
Science Fiction Research
    Association, 43, 49, 64
Science Fiction Writers of
    America, Inc., 32, 38, 43,
    48, 49, 53, 57–60, 62, 67,
    69, 79, 81, 90, 115, 121, 122,
    129
Scientific American, 16
Sci-fi, 1
S.f., 1
SFRA. *See* Science Fiction
    Writers Association
S.f./fantasy, 1
S.f./mystery, 6
SFPA. *See* Science Fiction
    Poetry Association
SFWA. *See* Science Fiction
    Writers of America, Inc.
SFWA Directory, 59
SFWA Forum, 48, 58–60, 69
SFWA Handbook, 58, 59
Shadows, 139
Signet, 147
Social sciences, 4
Society of Authors'
    Representatives, Inc., The,
    122
Soft s.f.
  definition, 3, 4
  examples, 9

Solar dynamics, 3
Songs, s.f., 27
Spacecraft, 3
Space opera
  definitions, 5
  examples, 10
Space Western
  definition, 6
Speculation, 5, 6
Speculative fiction
  definition, 5, 6
  examples, 10
Spock, Mr., 45
Starblaze—The Donning Co.
  Publishers, Inc., 148
"Star Trek" (TV), 44, 45, 53, 56
Star Wars, viii, 13, 14
*Starship: The Magazine About
  SF,* 68, 69
Sucharitkul, Somtow, 59
Sullivan, Eleanor, 137
Swank, 137
Sword & Sorcery
  definition, 4, 5
  example, 9, 10

T

TAFF. *See* Trans-Atlantic Fan
  Fund
Taplinger Publishing Co., 148
Technology, 2, 3
Terraforming, 3, 20
Themes and concepts, 20
Time machines, 3
Time travel, 2, 20
Timescape—Pocket Books, 148,
  149

Tor Books—Thomas Doherty
  Associates, 149
Tower Publications, Inc., 149
Trans-Atlantic Fan Fund, 45
Trekkies, 44, 45
Tribbles, 53
Trilby, David, 137
Triteness, 29, 30
Turner, Alice K., 137
"Twilight Zone" (TV), 135
2001: A Space Odyssey, 55
Typewriter hints, 77–78
Typing services, 78

U

Unique Graphics, 131
Universe, 138
Utopias, 20

V

Verne, Jules, 41
Viking Press, Inc., Publishers,
  The, 149
Vintage Books, 150

W

Wayne, Pierce, 136
Wells, H. G., 41
Westercon, 51
Western, 6
What if . . . , 17–19
Willden, Nye, 136
Wilson, Gahan, 63

Wollheim, Donald A., 143
Words, counting, 81–83
Workshops, 31, 32, 49
World Fantasy Award, 63
World Fantasy Convention, 54, 63
Worldcon, 38, 41, 45, 46, 51, 52, 54–56, 62, 63
Writer, The, 32, 34
Writers' and Artists' Yearbook, 35
Writer's Digest, 32, 34
Writer's Handbook, The, 34

Writer's Market, 34
Writer's Yearbook, 34
Writers Guild of America: East; West; Registration Service, 129
Writers, s.f., 38, 39, 42, 43, 47–49, 53, 54, 57–61, 63, 66
Writing Mysteries That Sell, 132

Z

Zebra Books, 150